2015 · **DRYLAND** · 2020

A LITERARY JOURNAL BORN IN SOUTH CENTRAL LOS ÁNGELES

5 YEARS

DRYLAND

MASTHEAD

FOUNDING EDITOR-IN-CHIEF/ BOOK DESIGNER
Viva Padilla

ASSISTANT EDITOR
Nikolai Garcia

EDITORIAL ASSISTANT
Amanda Orozco

ASSOCIATE WRITERS
Nidia Bautista
Jenise Miller
Michael Lorenzo Porter

INSIDE ART
Anthonyxyz
Giana De Dier
Biko Eisen-Martin (Postcard)
Iurhi Peña
Mr. Pintamuro
Michelle "La Mousie" Vega

COMMEMORATIVE PRINT DESIGNER
Hector Hernandez

COVER ART
"Racism Doesn't Rest During a Pandemic Pee Chee (No Justice No Peace)"
by Patrick Martinez

POETRY - FICTION - CREATIVE NONFICTION - ART - ISSUE 10 - JULY 2020 - LOS ANGELES
ISBN: 978-0-578-73681-5
COPYRIGHT © 2020 BY PONTE LAS PILAS PRESS
ALL RIGHTS RESERVED.

IG: @PONTELASPILASPRESS

DRYLANDLA.ORG

5TH ANNIVERSARY EDITION
DRYLAND ISSUE 10
FEATURING

WRITING BY:

NIDIA BAUTISTA
XOCHITL-JULISA BERMEJO
CAROLINA BLANCHARD
ANTHONY J. CASSARINO
JESSICA CEBALLOS Y CAMPBELL
JULIANA CHANG
ALAN CHAZARO
JESUS CORTEZ
ILIANA CUELLAR
JADE DANIELS
HOLLY DAY
ROBERTO DÍAZ
LINDA DOVE
OLGA GARCÍA ECHEVERRÍA
TONGO EISEN-MARTIN
AARON EL SABROUT
JO FODERINGHAM-BROWN
E.M. FRANCESCHINI
NIKOLAI GARCIA
TIMOTHY GOMEZ
JORDAN GREEN
LITUO HUANG
WILLIAM JOEL
ABRAHAM A. JOVEN
WASABI KANASTOGA
CLAIRE KOOYMAN
TEKA LARK
TRICIA LOPEZ
CHRISTIAN LOZADA
ALEXANDRA MARTINEZ
JENISE MILLER

BRIANA MUÑOZ
VIVA PADILLA
MICHAEL LORENZO PORTER
MONIQUE QUINTANA
EVA RECINOS
HENRY 7. RENEAU, JR.
LUIVETTE RESTO
TATIANA RETIVOV
BARBARA JANE REYES
KEVIN RIDGEWAY
NICK ROSSI
IVÁN SALÍ
RICK SMITH
SONDRIAWRITES
STEELE
MEI MEI SUN
MEGAN WARING
ARUNI WIJESINGHE
DEVYNITY WRAY
FERNANDO XÁUREGUI
HAOLUN XU

ART BY:

ANTHONYXYZ
GIANA DE DIER
BIKO EISEN-MARTIN
IURHI PEÑA
MR. PINTAMURO
MICHELLE "LA MOUSIE" VEGA

COVER ART BY:

PATRICK MARTINEZ

54th/Vermont Ave. across the street from Nativity Catholic School in South Central L.A.

Photo by Viva Padilla

Viva Padilla, Mariachi Plaza, July 2020

Photo by Nidia Bautista

EDITOR'S NOTE

IN PRE-K ON THE BUS BACK FROM A FIELD TRIP, MY CLASSMATE SITTING IN front of me started singing: "Siempre hay por quien vivir y a quien amar/ Siempre hay por que vivir por que luchar," a song by Julio Iglesias that my dad and his choir would sing as a (remixed) recessional song at Nativity Catholic Church on Sundays. I remember sitting back in my seat as the bus moved along, looking out the window and feeling the sun shine on me, as I listened to her sing. This is the first poem that ever stayed with me.

Growing up in the 90s, I went to a Catholic school that was founded by French nuns in 1925; it was a brick building in the middle of the hood (Slauson and Vermont Ave.) full of Black and Brown kids, and Black teachers.

During the '92 uprising, I remember hearing explosions in the distance outside my house and concluding as a little girl: *This is what war sounds like.* I remember it being my big brother's birthday, and my family and I were driving around looking for a place to have dinner, my parents unaware that riots were really happening right outside our door. I saw our carniceria off Martin Luther King Blvd completely black and gone. I remember worrying, "Where is the security man with black hair and a big black mustache?" He was a friend of my dad's who worked there, a Mexican with green eyes and a Chente look. After driving around more, we ended up in the parking lot of a KFC and my dad left all seven of us in the van as he went to go and check if it was open. He came back a while later, completely pale. As we pulled away, a Black guy came running toward the van with a baseball bat and my dad, the quick thinker, sped up towards him as if he were going to run him over. I remember we all went home after that and no one talked about anything. My dad later said that while inside the KFC, someone had pulled a gun on him.

I remember never having answers to these things I had experienced. My teachers never had them and neither did my dad or his cura friends, but I was embedded with the monastic love of studying and reading, that was impressed upon me by adults who taught me by example. It wasn't until I was later given a blank journal by my 6th grade teachers, Mr. Bender and Mr. Chen (my first non-Black teachers), I began to write within this journal's blank pages as a way to figure out my life, to ask all these questions no one seemed to have the answer for, questions that still seem unanswerable now. This is where *Dryland* was born.

A literary journal is a place for questions, a place where art can find you, where a personal narrative can be claimed and celebrated, shared and enjoyed by anyone who resonates with it. Literary journals should not be an unusual thing in our culture here in the US. They should not be saved for MFA programs and orgs with grantwriters backing it; they need to be in the hands of the people. Art comes to life within a soul that's ready to receive it. South Central (and communities like it) are, and have been, ready for it.

It's been 5 years since I started this journal. Before then, I had been on a path full of dead ends and false starts for a long while. Committing myself to *Dryland* has been in itself a commitment to save myself from all the forces that were close to constricting me to the self-destructive malaise of a ghetto, a historically racist creation, of South Central. By creating the journal, I trust that having this space that transcends a physical one, to share our ideas, our art, write our own stories, and ask the unanswerable questions—this is what will sustain us in the face of oppressive forces.

Dryland is a historical document, a way to claim our narrative. We are in our 10th issue and it feels like we are just starting. The number of contributors has doubled in comparison to issue 9, from 30 to almost 60. The support has been immense, and through the direct financial support from people (not grants or universities) we were able to publish 500 copies in our first print run. The writers who worked on pieces specifically for this issue, including Compton poet Jenise Miller and Boyle Heights reporter Nidia Bautista, are just a few of the brilliant voices in this issue. Shout-out to others featured in this issue: Tongo Eisen-Martin from the Bay, who shares the belief in our work and philosophy, Eva Recinos, a fellow South Central mujer who knows what having to be a jedi in training in the hood is like, and lastly Patrick Martinez (the cover artist), whose work I hope welcomes you to read us.

It is 2020. We are fumbling through this pandemic. History is on repeat. The cops have *barbarically* murdered a Black man on video… It's been a rough going in the past few months, to say the least, but this journal has been a lifeline for me, as I hope it is for others. Pausing it was never an option… because that song, that first poem that ever stayed with me, still resonates in my mind when it says, "there is always a reason to live, there is always a reason to fight."

—Viva Padilla

POEMS/POEMAS

SHORT FICTION

NONFICTION

ART + LIT INTERVIEWS

POEMS/POEMAS

AARON EL SABROUT

WILDFIRE.

I want to bathe you
in rosewater in a clearing
among the juniper trees.
It will be cold,
that I must promise you,
the mountain wind licking
across your skin
like cat tongues, rough
& scaly. Can we
consecrate this space
of *hazard* trees,
dry tinder waiting
to be animated
by a spark?

I walked across this land
5,000 years ago &
ancestors showed me
the seeds that only flower
when caressed by flame,
how water without fire
cannot make the desert bloom.

We watched explosions
across the dry plains at night,
celebrations, invasions, or disasters.
What do those men know about fire?
Have they stood in the crackling
chapparal as it burned & seen
the germ of life laid bare?

In a village clustered around an oasis
the spirit of the flame moved
through the palm trees & mouse dens
among the rocks. The water never rose
to save them because it knew:
the land must be burned clean
to grow again.

AARON EL SABROUT

NAVIGANT.

Black mesa full of flashing lights,
ten thousand villages on the hillside
all tchotchkes & finger-knit bracelets.
I walk in circles through the stale halls,
the "open air" over the mountain
across the valley in the land of
still juniper & fast rocks the land
waits for feet & water to push it along.
We can't fix it, the man will say
when you bring him the skipping
disk drives of our time. You'll have
to get a new one. It's a hardware
issue & we've all gone soft for
fluorescent lights & shopping bags.

What happens when the lights
can't guide us back anymore?
Which of us will shrug on
Orion's belt & cast their big
dipper into the dark water
of the sky to lead us home?

Are your ears ringing over there too?
Some days I can't hear anything
but the sounds in my own head;
the storage is full & no new data
can be saved to the disk.

Libra, point me out of this way,
I want starshine & the white
sage wind to blow through me
and all these trash can plastic cups—
I want to know the sunrise
from out beyond all this exhaust.

TONGO EISEN-MARTIN

I DO NOT KNOW THE SPELLING OF MONEY

I go to the railroad tracks
And follow them to the station of my enemies

A cobalt-toothed man pitches pennies at my mugshot negative

All over the united states, there are
                              Toddlers in the rock

I see why everyone out here got in the big cosmic basket
And why blood agreements mean a lot
And why I get shot back at

I understand the psycho-spiritual refusal to write white history or
take the glass freeway

                    White skin tattooed on my right forearm
                    Ricochet sewage near where I collapsed
                              into a rat-infested manhood

My new existence as living graffiti

                              In the kitchen with
                    a lot of gun cylinders to hack up
                              House of God in part
                              No cops in part

                    My body brings down the Christmas

The new bullets pray over blankets made from old bullets

Pray over the 28th hour's next beauty mark

Extrajudicial confederate statue restoration
the waist band before the next protest poster

                                        By the way,
                        Time is not an illusion, your honor
                          I will return in a few whirlwinds
                             I will save your desk for last
                               You are witty, your honor
                    You're moving money again, your honor

It is only raining one thing: non-white cops

              And prison guard shadows
                    Reminding me of
                    Spoiled milk floating on an oil spill

              A neighborhood making a lot of fuss over its
       demise

A new lake for a Black Panther Party

Malcolm X's ballroom jacket slung over my son's shoulders
                Pharmacy doors mid-slide
                        The figment of village
                a noon noose to a new white preacher
                Wiretaps in the discount kitchen tile
                                -All in an abstract painting of a
                president

Bought slavers some time, didn't it?
The tantric screeches of military bolts and Election-Tuesday cars

A cold-blooded study in leg irons
Leg irons in tornado shelters
Leg irons inside your body

Proof that some white people have fondled nooses
                That sundown couples
                made their vows of love over
                        opaque peach plastic
                        and bolt action audiences

Man, the Medgar Evers-second is definitely my favorite law of science

Fondled news clippings and primitive Methodists

My arm changes imperialisms
Simple policing vs. Structural frenzies
Elementary school script vs. Even whiter white spectrums

Artless bleeding and
the challenge of watching civilians think

"terrible rituals they have around the corner. They let their elders
beg for public mercy...beg for settler polity"

"I am going to go ahead and sharpen these kids' heads into arrows
myself and see how much gravy spills out of family crests."

Modern fans of war
What with their t-shirt poems
And t-shirt guilt

And me, having on the cheapest pair of shoes on the bus,
I have no choice but to read the city walls for signs of my life

TONGO EISEN-MARTIN

I MAKE PROMISES BEFORE I DREAM

No unclaimed, cremated mothers this year

Nor collateral white skin

No mothers folding clothes to a corporate park preamble
No sons singing under the bright lights of a lumber yard

Quantum reaganomics and the tap steps of turning on a friend

New York trophy parts among
  the limbs of decent people
   Being an enraged artist is like
    entering a room and not knowing what to get high off of

  My formative symbols/My upbringing flying to an agent's ears
         I might as well be an activist

       Called my girlfriend and described
  All the bottles segregationists had thrown at me that day

   Described recent blues sites and soothing prosecutions
         I feared for my poetry

You have to make art every once in a while
    While in the company of sell-outs
    Accountant books in deified bulk
    Or while waiting for a girl under a modern chandelier

        Or in your last lobby as a wanderer

            The prison foot races the museum

              My instrument ends

    I mean, what is a calendar to the slave?
        Also, what is a crystal prism?

              "He bought this bullet,
                bought its flight,
            then bought two more"

KALIEF BROWDER

Rest in Power, Kalief Browder, oil on canvas, by Anthonyxyz

HAOLUN XU

FIRST MEMORY

I am born
like a bad gamble,
With my mother downstairs
recovering from her first C-section.

This is the first impact I make. I cry and I cry.
I think that's my father in front of me.
I can't see his face.
Next to him is an angel.

Lay there as long as you want.
No one is mad at you. No one will blame you.
Welcome, to the world. You've got all the time,
so much time in front of you.

I ask, will it hurt?
I am sorry. I am very very sorry.
I cannot promise anything.
But I do have stories. I can tell you a story.

I'm waiting for the story.
Only one shadow stands in front of me now.
I wonder if it's the angel or my father,
I wonder who will pick me up.

I hear a voice for just a bit before falling back asleep.
With the clock ticking,
The hand starts to rewind,
and I fall asleep to the spaces between each second.

ALEXANDRA MARTINEZ

SOMEWHERE

Outside the library
all the jobless are walking around
staying out of the shade,
out of the embrace of the
Santa Ana winds.
It's 2 o'clock and the clocktower plays
"Somewhere" from *West Side Story*
There's the couple I always see
The man shuffles in front of the woman
as she pushes their home along.
They don't notice
all the painted ladies
swarming around and how they
flutter slowly like falling confetti
inside the Staples Center.
Slowly,
like a migration.
The couple
does a loop around the park
and starts another one.
Peace and quiet and open air
Butterflies know nothing
of walls and fences and borders.
I wish for the couple the luck of butterflies
Somehow, someday, somewhere.

Me molesta la ciudad, Chinese ink on paper, by Iurhi Peña

ALEXANDRA MARTINEZ

OCEAN

In Puerto Rico there's a beach that's surrounded by a rock wall
if you look at videos online you'll see there was a time where the
ocean could crash over the rock wall and water would come in and
fill into a half moon beach below but when I was there climate
change had done away with that it was still possible to climb atop
the black volcanic rock so I did that and all I could see was miles
and miles of waves it felt colder up there and the wind was so
strong that it was hard to stand up straight I made my way up
higher on the sharp jagged rocks and watched a young boy stare
out at the sea I could hear "Ocean" by The Velvet Underground
playing in my head and felt that kind of rush you feel when you're
exhilarated to be alive but also astounded at the easy opportunity
to just end it all

JULIANA CHANG

MOM'S MAKEUP

mom's makeup for your senior prom
mom with the eyeliner and the red red lips
mom who knows a lady for everything
mom buys you a bra before you got boobs
she thinks it can be aspirational
mom and the fading tattooed eyebrows
mom loves Jennifer Aniston, won't watch any movies with Brad Pitt
for years after the divorce, mom asking for a *People* magazine
every time you fly home
mom zooming in on every group photo to see if she blinked
mom calling it a good photo if she didn't, even if every other
face is blurry.
mom so sad that you can't share shoes
mom thinks it's funny your feet are tiny
mom says you would've married well in the Tang dynasty
mom says *don't marry someone like your dad*
says *love is usually a mistake*

mom like tough-tongued immigrant like
mom spitting broken glass english at the Marshalls saleslady
ripped her off
mom doesn't care if she can't pronounce *Estée Lauder*
mom filling the whole store with her accent
mom gets the blush and perfume for free, of course.
mom is ice cold when she meets your boyfriend
mom yells more than she wants
mom alone for holidays more than she wants
mom so tired of all the business trips
mom and blotchy cheeks on your 5th birthday
mom with the good foundation and smooth smooth concealer
mom never aging in the photos, just in her eyes.

mom hard as in mom never soft.
mom wouldn't know soft if it called her on the phone
like an old friend.
mom would probably ask soft what pyramid scheme
they were trying to run and hang up before
soft could answer. mom has never been soft,
but she is
wearing Juicy sweatpants, filling the house
with the smell of rice and scrambled eggs
the morning of your 7th christmas.

mom with the wobbly heels and the big big voice
mom with the seven-year-old and the toddler in tow:
she marches into toys-R-us on christmas day
haggles with the sales associate alone.

E.M. FRANCESCHINI

CARACOLES

since we all live and die by myths
I choose the myth of red corn

because those whose hands touch the soil
know everything there is to know
and there can never be enough names for *mother*

so when I asked him if he, too, had made his choice
he sketched a black mask
then,
one braid after the next, weaved a milpa of red corn
into every next step he would ever take

leaving in my throat the echo of the snail's song:

para todos *todo*
para nosotros *nada*

FERNANDO XÁUREGUI

PU-PU-SA

pu

pu

s

a

te

acepto

[comunión cotidiana]

[sacra]

[arrodillado ante vos]

[mi maíz]

[mi dios]

[mi vos]

a mi plato

me

xi

co

a

me

ri

ca

no

[pocho]

mesoamérica [me invade][invisible][ingiero] [con manos] [labios] y [vos]

FERNANDO XÁUREGUI

SUDAR...

sudar

a propósito

repartir momentos
intercalar claroscuros

Injertar palabras

Transformar lo norte
en sur,
agotarse en lo zurdo

hacer de la confusión
un éxtasis,

el estado de aquí:

you know

being heavy and strong

light and

leaving

returning
comenzaron   again

"hablas demasiado"

naces cimarrón
más estúpida más superflua
más placentera más fricción

INCOMPLETA

incumplida sin reloj
yemas húmedas

la boca

come piedras

the word in your mouth is   *anarchy*

WASABI KANASTOGA

SNEAKERS HANGING ON ELECTRICAL WIRES

He points his gun at me, a plastic model I recognize from the thrift stores. I raise my arms high above my head. My shirt stretches out from my pants. His hand is steady, but the face trembles with anger.

"Keep 'em higher mother fuck," he warns with calm deadness in his eyes. He could press that trigger and riddle me with plastic bullets, then go home to a calm late afternoon cartoon. I step back onto the street,

cars brush my back side. A helicopter hovers. His attention shifts. Sneakers hanging on electrical wires sway with the wind from the chopper's blades. The boy drops his gun and begins to hurl dirt clods

at the chopper. The chunks barely make it above the wires, then splatter onto the pavement. I keep walking back, hands down. He has forgotten about me. I reach my car. Turn on the engine. The

chopper continues its mid-air dance like a giant metal fly hovering over death, the L.A. Sheriff's insignia on its side. I drive off.

BARBARA JANE REYES

BROWN GIRL HUSTLE

Grind
I see you, running from job to job, hustling up shit-stained esca-
lators. Your discount store black patent comfort shoes are killing
your feet. You're boarding the train invaded by white manspread-
ing assholes. You're elbowing your way through turnstiles and
messenger-bagged tech bros, you're sardining into piss-rank bus-
es. This is where you're eating your lunch. You'll forget to reapply
your lipstick. Your eyebrow wax is two weeks overdue; what a
mess your face is. You're graying. You don't have time for color
correction. I see you fingering your hemline. You're thinking your
skirt's a tad too short. Your control top pantyhose is starting to
run. Your hair bun's coming undone. I need to tell you I see you.
You're never not running. You're never not working. They act as
if you are not even here. They erase you. But I see you. Yes, I see
you. I know it'll be dark when you sit, just for a minute in the
kitchen, when you take a deep breath, when you begin again.

Playaz
See us? We are the last Pinays standing, in this smoke-stained
place, the bourbon no better than high lead level tap water. If
there are still jukeboxes filled with scratched 45s, they belong
right here. We're young but not too young, we're out past curfew.
Your eyes see little brown ball-bangers in this valley of tables. You
peek down our blouses, you press up as we bend. We know we got
you beat, man. Our shots are clean, we kiss only when we mean.
Go ahead, break. Your body english tells us we'll be sinking gold.
Halika, see what we can do with this stick.

Ana (Swing)
See how we do not tap out. We slide our way out of your hold. We

spring back up when you sucker punch. We bite down so hard, our mouths break tin and tart inside. When we get back up, you mispronounce our names. Still. We'll correct you, sometimes. We all pick our battles. When we speak up, you step back, big stance. We bend our knees, we open our hips. Pivot, and there's our left jab in your jaw. We bob and weave, we block and swing. Right cross, left hook. We are not too dainty for this grappling and grounding. We don't care if you don't like what we're wearing. We'll take you down, we'll choke you out. And then we'll walk.

Pia (Queen)

Brother, see how I roll lumpias wearing this tiara, this much mascara, and my fave black super skinny jeans. I shoot selfies with millionaire ballers. They are starstruck in my sequined glow. My eyebrows are so sharp, they slice you so clean, you don't have time to remember to bleed. I sprint up your mountains in my five-inch pumps. I trained myself in seven. I leave you in the dust.

I step into the room; elders' looms get clacking. Clopping cobblestone. Swishing silk. And how my genteel countrymen swoon. My jusi couture, my capiz shell terno, my siete cuchillos, if only María Clara could have cut with these. My evening gown's a river plunging, you cannot fathom its depth. Gemstones shined by typhoon, by rush, by the rawest force of will.

You cannot airbrush me. There is no need. You cannot translate me. I command your tongue. I thwack your knuckles with my curling iron, when you do not step back. I sing karaoke, loud, and off key. No, you really cannot quiet me.

BARBARA JANE REYES

[REMEMBER THOSE DIARIES WE WERE GIFTED]

DEAR BROWN GIRL,

Remember those diaries we were gifted as young girls, pale pink and floral, embossed with golden curlicues. Remember that tiny golden lock and precious key. Remember wanting to crawl inside and hide there. Remember how not speaking yielded so many secrets. Remember how you'd write and write, like if you didn't write, you would just die. Like if anyone ever read what you wrote, you would just die. They'd say, artista ka talaga, 'susmaryosep, anak. And you'd cry. Of course you'd cry.

Remember when you were nineteen, your poems were so honey coated. Your language was not really your language. It was so sugary, fancy and high. You wrote about things you didn't know how to write about. Nineteen-year-old girl living on Top Ramen and minimum wage, remember how you blew a whole paycheck on a Waterman Laureat mineral blue fountain pen, and tender purple ink, how you transcribed your finished poems into the matching hardbound, violet marbled journal edged with gold leaf. You loved that scratch of gold-plated nib onto paper. You gazed at each glossy page air-drying before you turned the page or closed the book.

Dear Brown Girl, nobody ever read your poems back then. And then again, none of those poems were for them, di ba?

BARBARA JANE REYES

TRACK: "SOULFUL DRESS," SUGAR PIE DESANTO (1964).

We'll shake and we shout 'til morning and roar.
No, there's nothing tamed about us, not the hemline,
not the neckline, not this streak of red lipstick,
not these shit kickers. Nothing silent, nothing shy,
nothing here but fly. Nothing asking nothing from you,
'cept, get outta our way, 'cept this is no ask.
Don't tell us to dial it down. Don't tell us to be ladies.
We'll show you our teeth. Don't lecture that we reckless,
just recognize. You step the fuck back son, and you recognize.

To Be Your One, pencil on bristol paper, by Michelle "La Mousie" Vega

HENRY 7. RENEAU, JR.

EXPLAIN YOURSELF

covered up in sorrow, but convincingly burning like a star,
a fearless poem,

trying to explain
how unjust the world is, in one thousand & one words.

its child-like pout, a bomb that's been ticking there
too long: the silent screams of deferred dreams, resisting

the mandated Order with chants & bottles & rocks,
cascading onto armored tanks mowing through non-violent

protesters, to impose order & laws that must be obeyed.
the riot squads polishing their bullets, dreading

the rabble dressed in Sunday-best rebellion, the whirlwind
within the chaos of designated fear.

a noble poem,
enshrined within the gobble & gluttony of status quo illusion.

the brutal events that transpired there are still not
entirely known: the orphaned, screaming, war-child amputees &

a Muslim-American officer accused of serial spree kill.
the brilliant capture & distraction of light: a matter of semantics

that becomes a fabrication, the perfect place
to hide a deployment of greed that unravels into euphemism—

the innocent civilians massacred—into collateral damage.
a visionary poem,

searching for the meaning of truth to fill a begging space,
the buried-in-the-mud vacuum of mass graves

interlocking tendon & nerve & bone.
the fathomless hate & discordant rhetoric—the persistent deceit.

a strident poem
convincingly burning like a star.   those wayward activists

subject to prosecution: the UC Davis Mrak 5-1.   like the
Chicago Seven
in lieu of Bobby Seale   or Harriet Tubman, et. al.

those few fearless   alarming comfort zone regimentation into
disarray—
the labeled *Other*.

a cautionary poem: don't believe the government, the sound bite lies,
or anything on FOX News.

the wolf amongst the sheep, pretending to be something else:
                                                    we only did it

to bring *them* salvation through blue-eyed Jesus, to bring them
freedom &

democracy.   we did it in the name of Progress.   to civilize them,
to oust the foreign terrorist-sponsoring despot—to balance

the national budget.
                    hellfire &

save the matches!!
we only did it . . . because we could.

Jesus Noir, oil on canvas, by Anthonyxyz

HENRY 7. RENEAU, JR.

PLANTATION LULLABIES,
OR THE POLITICS OF DANCING

It's a brand new dance / but I don't know its name —David Bowie

Poets refuse to read from the teleprompter // Their choice of words/ a
streetlight burning daylight
on the corner of Hope St. & Chance/ or the strewn facets of
storefront glass/ glimmering diamond-like black asphalt velvet //

The rebellion by attrition // Unraveling/: the hell no! stance
of Rosa Parks/ or

Patti Smith in person/ at the Licorice Pizza record store/ strangely magical &
reckless // The brazen indecency of her sound/ her unfettered energy/
every inch the glam gothic crow/: the dauntless reckoning of her weight/ a
random chaos of Furies wreathed in the eccentricities of genius/ or the milli-

second gap in time/   it takes the fire to follow the fuse/   from the detonator/
to kaboom!!

/exhaling the facticity
of what comes from within/: 56 poems of prophecy
as cocky the predictions of Muhammad Ali //
The non-violent   *kiss my white ass!*   /of Joan Trumpauer Mulholland //

The 24 hr. news cycle/   like fire
reflected in shards of broken glass //   The vetted PR version
& redacted omissions
/of po-lice body cams &
dash cams   (*may be too graphic for some viewers*)   /is what
we are told to believe //   The repeated video
of lies/   *the best way to break a body without damaging the shell*   /&
the cloned slew of guest experts/   every hour   /on the hour //

It is not surprising/ how little anyone really knows/ about anything //

The only way out/ is to wake the fuck up/:

Everything comes down so pasteurized . . .

like a clock . . .
tic / toc tic / toc tic / toc

fuck the clock!

I awakened, & smelled something burning, living
as a moving target
inside the imperial Amerikkkan Flying Machine. My joy
as happenstance as an insect trapped in a glass.

I always assumed it was because I am Black, the déjà vu feel
of repeated history
we were born into, & not expected to survive. The whispers
become an awkward silence when I enter a room, & I realize
I'm the token Black invited.

I learned at a young age
that the best way to survive the po-lice
is to smile excessively
so that I don't look threatening, be deferential,
& speak so slowly that I cannot be misunderstood, as if
I were speaking to small children, who were still learning the language

/: Hands. Up. Don't. Shoot.

We been assailed
until we could no longer be who we are/: how do you explain
that you actually did something
that a racist would assume you were likely to end up doing anyway?

This is how the mute button works/ the rats-in-the-wall
sound of fear, like saucer wide eyes &
grief-hungry mouths

/: I.   Can't.   Breathe.

We contort adaptively.   Entangle ourselves
huddled in safe spaces/:   in-between uppity   & until the revolution come

& every day, I am less
& less afraid.

ALAN CHAZARO

POSTCARD FROM ACAPULCO

The night here is taking me

towards an eternity, towards

an unbuttoning, somewhere

beneath oiled palm leaves, beneath

the mouth of sea drizzle. I'm standing

near an emptied street, inside the crooked

hands of God. I'm looking

down from this roof, observing

a city of wet and blurred

yellows. In the distance, further

than I can navigate

with my eyes, an open beach.

The gravel is thickening

between yesterday and

tomorrow. Wake me up

when I've reached peace,

when I've mapped these ruins

and star patterns. When I've tongued

coconuts and danced reggaeton

with el Espíritu Santo. I will leave

with sand in my pockets, with a jungle

I cannot untangle in my throat.

MEI MEI SUN

WHAT IS LOVE?

Love is watered-down orange juice. Love is a filthy green truck. The sad, red whirr of an uncharged electronic. Love is as thick as thieves. Food so rich with soul it gave you heart attacks. Love is something too good to overstay its welcome. An infestation of ladybugs. Love is never washing your hair in the winter. The unexpected and unwanted dinner guest. Love is a long-recalled metal pin. A little golden bear full of honey. Love is two geckos on your nightstand. Cows slaughtered to be made into dollar-store steak. Love is a half watermelon eaten over the kitchen sink. Love is a blood-drunk mosquito. An unexpected seizure at midnight. Love is the dark blue vest of a hotel manager. A night in western Mongolia. Love is a grocery-store fish tank. A dumb, media-made label. Love is a blue Swiss lake. Love is an angry voicemail. The toys of men who know better. Love is an eighth-grade midnight tryst. Love is a continental breakfast. The child of a debt collector. Love is never meeting your heroes. Love is the stilled Atlantic. Love is an alcoholic vegan. Love is only a zip code away – ~~click here.~~

ARUNI WIJESINGHE

IF JUDY BLUME WAS MY AUNT

Her name would be
my middle name
instead a Sanskrit word
for a flower that doesn't grow
in New York City.

At family parties
I would sit with her
while she'd sneak Virginia Slims.
We'd skip the rice and curry, steal away
 to McDonald's for burgers and Cokes.

I'd finally have
the life I checked out
of the school library,
the simplicity of meatloaf dinners
and Shaun Cassidy records.

She'd give me
a soft-focus adolescence
and the reassurance that I would
eventually bud, my body flowering
on its own mysterious schedule.

She'd gift me a diary,
tell me to start with lists
of boys' names, streets, colors:
Andrew Mallon, the two Aldo Leones,
Revere Place, Howard Avenue, Lester Drive,
dogwood pink —

these lists would become my answers.

OLGA GARCÍA ECHEVERRÍA

BENDITO DÍA QUE TE FUISTE

Fuiste una gran grosería
Una comemierda presidencial
Una alabanza a la tiranía
Fuiste
Fuiste un títere triste en Twitter

Te valió madre la tierra
Te valió menos el pueblo

Encarcelaste a niños

Violaste a mujeres
Violaste a la justicia
a la verdad
al país

Bendito día que te fuiste
Fuiste
Fuiste una gran grosería
Un golpe al estado
Un asalto diario
Un tiroteo de insultos
Un payaso en poder que hizo y deshizo
y aún nunca pudo algo bueno hacer

Bonito día que te fuiste
Cuando caíste al piso como pierdas[1]
hasta los ateos dieron gracias a Dios
Los refugiados del mundo aplaudieron
Por todos lados nuestras lágrimas de alegría cayeron
Llenaron lagos llenaron rios llenaron mares
Celebramos con piñatas y garrotes
Con deliciosos tacos en cada pinche esquina
Con conjuntos inmigrantes
Con un pastel enorme hecho por el Sindicato de Panaderos Gay
Y por todos lados se cantaba
Y Por todos lados se oía

Queremos pastel pastel pastel

---

[1] Una alusión a la muerte del muy corupto personaje Pedro Páramo en el libro *Pedro Páramo* por Juan Rulfo.

CHRISTIAN LOZADA

SAN PEDRO:
VOTED THE L.A. COUNTY'S SURLIEST CITY

What did we do to get this designation?
Was it the middle-aged woman at the bus stop
waiting
drinking a naked 40?
Does she make this city surly
or does she drink to deal with the surliness?
Is it the tatted up at Peck Park or Point Fermin
playing horseshoes or bocce
surrounded by bushes and gutters littered with used condoms?
Is it the gas leaks from the refineries,
the salt from the sea,
the smell of carne asada wafting through the hills?
These things don't say surly to me.
They are a vote,
a stake
to still love violently and desperately all
all the things that might, maybe, may get you through the day.
Fuck your surly.
We only love in the ways we have been shown.

CHRISTIAN LOZADA

MY WHITE BROTHER CAN'T FIND A JOB

My Filipino one can't find one either.
I can explain one but not the other.
I can explain one but not the other.
My Filipino brother tells the bosses he's Hispanic
       even though he's not
My white brother tells the bosses he's Filipino
       because he is
I don't know why either says these things
I don't know why either says these things
It's as if there is advantage to be on a lower rung
and my white brother silently screams his brownness:
       ignore my skin,
       I am more than this
And my Filipino brother silently screams his otherness:
       accept me for what I am not
       because I don't trust what I am
I can explain one but not the other
I can explain one but not the other

TATIANA RETIVOV

TO TAMARA IN ROCK CREEK

Tamara, you are more alive than before.
The cushions on your fingers are still
waiting for love. Aunt Emma questions
your whereabouts, the time of your return.
Patiently she reads the Holy Book
all day remembering your smile.

If you were back, it would be
no different. The same tug-of-war
between mate and mate on an uncarved tomb
waiting for your surrender.
When you were found in the ruins
of their unyielding passion, it was too late.

Tamara, if you had never gone, I would be
the one you would pay homage to.
You too would wonder what,
for heaven's sake,
there is to do
when dying's done by others.

Still, you are gone. The marble dome
that shelters you is cold.
Sometimes the watchman hears me racing
for the moon at dawn. I come to weed.
The parsley has grown brown
around the corners of your bed.

ILIANA CUELLAR

JOCOTE

marking the passage of time
ripening at the pace of colibrí
wings and the colors marked
outlining the large fig leaves
against a setting sun

needing the flames
to sprout new growth
the sullen smokiness
fills the air and
fertilizes the earth

sinewy branches hug
each other and never
mind the leaves as the
bulbous fruit hang low
begging to be eaten

drop a handful
in my palms
the wax on the skin
fills my fortune lines

obscuring the past
where returning is
always a myth

JORDAN GREEN

COCAINE AND TAFFY

Like powdered knuckles
On Sunday evenings,
Love's a lark,
It watches you practice mom's eulogy,
She's the reason you wore
That white vest
To picture day as a child,
Two missing buttons under the collar
Matched the gap in your teeth,

The girl you liked
Laughed when she saw you,
That's her way of saying
You look good
But not good enough,
She's bound for a high school pregnancy,
You've got a bone to pick with mom
The embalming's made her flexible

Maybe you're like dad
Looking for that Lark,
Because cocaine gets cold,
Killing the wood
Before it gets to her inner hearth,
He called mom Taffy,
It gave him something to chew on
After washing the powder
Off his knuckles for a bump of chicken,

Looking at those hands
Darker than yours
Remembering he's in the kitchen,
Writing a sweet eulogy for his Taffy,
He's got to stop dreaming of winter
When winter's not dreaming of him,
He's says "find your sweetness buddy"
You think of Picture Day girl
Fat with another man's cocaine,

Dad's hands
They're whiter than yours now,
You leave, tired of larks,
From the front yard
You see mom's head
Peeking out the upstairs window,
She's just hanging there,
The window's closed and
She's just hanging there.

HOLLY DAY

FRACTURED

I close the lid of the makeup case
put it away. There are too many dreams
imaginary lessons of how to use lipstick and blush
to ever want to do my own face again.
the blues and pinks in the case are only
for little girls
that will never be.

I thumb through the photographs, wonder
if these days are worth remembering
if it's better to pretend I never
posed by a crib in a maternity dress
holding a pink teddy bear destined only
for rummage sales and a stranger's child.

HOLLY DAY

THE FLOOD

The coffins float to the surface
like rebellious architecture, buoyed by the floodwaters
that have shaken everything loose. We pass sandbags
hand over hand to build a wall between us and the river
shouting panicked instructions to the trucks to bring more.

The water pouring in from the river is frigid and cold
numbing ankles and hands, but the water
running off of the bloated cemetery is warm, as though the water
is carrying the last breath and embrace of the dead
across the grounds to keep us from freezing.

HOLLY DAY

THE BOOK BONFIRE, OF WHICH I WAS NOT A PART BUT HEARD ABOUT THE NEXT DAY

The books burn quickly, fill the air with the burning
of tiny insects and mildew spores, ancient glue and
cracked leather. Words glow bright on pages before
paper catches fire, being of a more conductive medium.

You could almost read the stories as they exploded with light, if you
could just freeze the moment of time between the pages first heating
up and finally catching fire. In the dark, large-print titles flash

JO FODERINGHAM-BROWN

OUT OF MANY/ONE PEOPLE

"You from home?" the man asked
And I didn't realize what he meant at first
Because I was at work and we were busy
But then the accent clicked
And then I noticed his hand was pointed towards the
sticker on my laptop
Which reads "likkle but tallawah"
In a circle around a flag of green black and gold
Framed by doctor birds
And I told him I was born here but
Yes, my entire family is from home
He asked where and I said Clarendon
Specifically, from May Pen
He told me he is from St. Ann
And that his father taught at Mona
We talked about our strange, foreign family names
Which are not from our small island
He did not treat me like an American
Though I said I was born in Atlanta
But yes, I thought
Three hours later as I was frying plantain
Yes, I am from home.

ミスターピンタムロ

Patlani, graphite pencil on paper, edited digitally, by Mr. Pintamuro

IVÁN SALÍ

VALLEYS

I come from   another valley where
                                         aztec ruins float

over-crowded lakes—   and sacrificed
                                         poor students flee

not too far from   militarized cities
                                         trapping us in-between

colonized hills;   under the sun
                                         I thought I left my valley behind—

in the drying suburbs   where the natives work
                                         in warehouses and on supermarkets

oranges are the only fruit,   I miss you
                                         but did I ever leave?

I still thirst   during your droughts
                                         lighting up my apartment on

fire in September and   I am still not independent.
                                         From your white picket fences

I can imagine   you sending me
                                         my social security

arriving safely   in the mail
                                         at risk of being stolen

TEKA LARK

THOSE PEOPLE'S NEIGHBORHOODS

Somebody tried to steal my neighborhood
They moved in and built a big fence and put up cameras
They asked me whose family I worked for
"I am sorry. I am so embarrassed."

Somebody tried to steal my neighborhood
They moved in and bought a rescue pit bull and then another one
They walked around with both of them and never said hi to anyone,
not even once
"I like dogs. Dogs are nicer than people."

Somebody tried to steal my neighborhood
They moved in and said the church service was too loud
They called the cops—and the cops came
"I believe in science. I need quiet to meditate on Sunday mornings."

Somebody tried to steal my neighborhood
They moved in and opened an art gallery
They got interviewed on that big blog
"I am happy to bring art to this 'underserved' community."

Somebody tried to steal my neighborhood
They moved in and opened a coffee shop
They didn't like our protest
"I am not racist. People are ignorant, the first coffee was brewed by
Ethiopians, so how are we racist? Understand history."

Somebody tried to steal my neighborhood
They moved in and started an Instagram account
They typed they were w-a-i-t-i-n-g 2 g-e-t -s-h-o-t- :) :) :)
"I think this place is so edgy."

Somebody tried to steal my neighborhood
They started ordering food, lots of it
They started complaining about the people delivering the food
"I don't like these e-bikes. Bicycles are about exercise. If you
don't want to do your job safely you should quit."

Somebody tried to steal my neighborhood
They moved in and they started a business
They started serving rosé wine in 40-ounce style bottles (you get
it right, I didn't get it either must be a somebody joke)
"I am a trailblazer. I moved here first."

Somebody tried to steal my neighborhood
They moved in and then the city opened a school, to relieve 'over-
crowding' because the local school
was 'overcrowded'
They made it hard to get in
"I want the best for my children. Don't you want the best for your
children?"

Somebody tried to steal my neighborhood
They moved in and said the ice cream truck was too loud
They went to the community board
"I know that has to be illegal. It isn't reasonable to expect me to
endure that noise."

Somebody tried to steal my neighborhood
They moved in, well they bought a house
They Airbnb'd it
"I know you hear 'random POC neighborhood' but it's very nice.
You'd be surprised."

MEGAN WARING

CROSS-COUNTRY PAUSE

There is an infestation in Billings,
Montana of bunnies, milling about
like they own the town. Said to be killing
off gardens, harvest thieves. Let out years ago
by a dying man. But his breed survived:
lays on the summer asphalt, soaks the sun,
becoming kings, breeding, feasting, thriving.
We see them as we pour between bars, run
after them, hazy day-drunk, oasis
from the car, the flat, the doubt. When you pass
your three drink maximum, we think of places
we could live. *Maybe here!* Lipstick smears on your glass,
clink beers. A bunny steps over train tracks. Today
feels like we'll make it. We've already made it halfway.

ABRAHAM A. JOVEN

WHERE ARE YOU FROM?

I come from a land that's foreign to your
Blue eyes. Tin roofs and cardboard thatches,
Old newsprint patching the holes
Where cheap cinderblock has worn away.
A tri-level housing three generations of
Aguinaldos; gifts and a legacy. Both.
Where the diesel mixes with the humidity and steamed rice
To form a unique smell that settles on you
Like a heavy comforter.

I also come from a desert:
Where my islander lungs struggle against the parched
Air and my people thirst for peace, and justice,
And fresh produce. Where a three bedroom
Apartment houses three generations of
PlayStations and yet
Feels empty. Especially during the holidays -
Especially during pasko where there are
No parols on our block except ours
No one eating adobo in their homes except ours
And no grandfather to bless or hug or tell you
That he loves you the way Nick's tells him
In every birthday card.

I am from the space between.

ABRAHAM A. JOVEN

MACARTHUR RETURNED

My people have a weird fascination with
General Douglas MacArthur.
I asked my mom about it once and
In classic immigrant parent stoicism
Said: "He said he'd come back and
He did."
The implication:
"MacArthur *actually* returned
To our little speck in the Pacific. Imagine!"

I wonder what he did after he left
While my grandfather's friends were
Reduced to machine gun fodder
And this collection of languages
Ferried by colorful Jeepneys
Underneath the precious shade of dahon
Wrapped in the rich smell of roasting lechón
Reveling in the delicate crunch of lumpia
Taking in the refreshing taste of calamansi
All belonging to America
Coveted in ways my people couldn't ignore
Until suddenly we weren't worth the bother.
Weren't worth the cost of American lives.
Clearly too much.

And so, I wondered about what he did while he was gone.
Because he sure as shit didn't retreat to America
To tell of us. To prepare the way
So the kids at my elementary school wouldn't look confused when
I told them of where I'm from.
Might as well have been Gondor.
Might as well just call you Japanese.
You're all the same.

I know he didn't speak of us
Cause these Americans called me "chink" and
Couldn't find the Philippines on a map and
Couldn't even find the time to give my grandfather and
His surviving friends the citizenship they'd paid for
In blood and sweat.
Carrying instead
The burden of the memories
Of a home they'll never return to
While never quite outpacing
The ceaseless phantoms of the ones
That didn't make it.

And I guess my thing is, if he didn't leave to tell the world about us
Then he left cause we weren't worth saving.

MacArthur *actually* returned
Like my deadbeat father:
After all the hard stuff, hand out,
Expecting a hero's welcome.

JADE DANIELS

SINCE I BEEN BORN

Since I been born—

The world been telling me
What they think is best

I think it's best you just be quiet
I think it's best you just sit down
I think it's best you change yourself completely
And don't make a fucking sound
Go and Disappear until I need you
And you better not be late.

I think it's best you do ALL this work and labor - and no you
won't get paid
And we think it best you not complain or
need breaks
or rest or a thanks
for your stress

I really think it's best
That you never yearn for freedom or seek autonomy-
douse out all that fire
that lives in ya chest

You should stay shackled here with me
You won't ever get the time you need
To figure it out for yourself

Why?
Because that's what I
think is best.

I think it best
You just listen to me
And act accordingly
I think it's best you don't challenge my authority
I think it's best you just agree with me
I think it best you don't ask for accountability
Shut the fuck up and listen
While I tell you about yourself
Your family
Your heart mind and intentions
I think it's best
That you dance for me

Care and entertain these niggas
Yea
And you know
I definitely think it best you
never say no
When I wanna fuck
When I wanna touch
or stare
or abuse
Or do some random shit
To prove my power over you.
Internalize all my projections
Cause they ARE the gospel truth

Just be quiet and sit down somewhere

And don't even think about
Asking for justice or support or retribution
Don't speak to your dead
That's all an illusion
No need to know your history
Yeah definitely not that
There's too much there
For you to ever unpack

I think it would be best
For you to just die
I should be the one to kill you
To make sure you don't survive

Yes, maybe that's best

But not until
I get what I need
And only after
You fuck me
Yes yes
O Trust me,
I think that's what's best
....

And I be like, nah.

(a poem about you weirdos)

Un poco peda, un chingo violenta, digital ink, by Iurhi Peña

LITUO HUANG

CONTRAPUNTAL DIVINE

is the God of stars	the same God of text messages
the God of biopsies	is the God of my promotion
the God that smites	the minor God is
the so-called major God	the God of petals
is the God of calamities	that God incubates
so I no longer pray to	this little God of little things
any real God at all	is all I need

JESSICA CEBALLOS Y CAMPBELL

TONIGHT, I'M BOTH AT HOME, AND FAR FROM IT.
OR WE LEAVE AND WE STAY, ALL AT ONCE,
OR NOT AT ALL
OR THE SEVEN THINGS I LEARNED FROM MY FATHER.

1. We are not the papers we are not born with.

2. We are the constellation, born as the shape of the sun.

3. We are not the places we come from,

4. we are the places we mourn.

5. Like dancing, the weeping of mourning can carry a home.

6. Or, it can carry the houses we abandon, whichever weighs less.

7. We are whatever weighs more.

BRIANA MUÑOZ

GENTE

Bartender (who got her BA in Spanish Lit)
Reading Lorca at an open mic,
With her hand in her back pocket,

Whittier street juggler,
With a bow tie and striped socks

"I thought they only do this at La Linea
As folks wait to cross back."

Old man feeding L.A. street pigeons
At a bus stop
Like it's his day job,

Mariachi woman
At Mariachi Plaza,

"You belong there, just as much as they do."

Man who asked me for change on my way to work,
Man who asked me for change in the parking lot,
Woman with knotted hair
Who was yelling
In front of Burrito King,
In Echo Park on a Saturday night

"I wish I had more to give."

Child who hustles chocolate bars
To support his basketball team, field trip,

Artist selling his mixtape
In Venice Beach,
Like it's still 1998,

Paletero man,
Tamale woman
Pupusa-selling-grandmother
At the mat

"It is tempting, pero soy vegetariana."

Aztec dancers
At Ruben Salazar Park
With chachayotes wrapped around ankles
Which resemble
Tree leaves shaking

"Your dancing is healing our universe."

Punk kids
Hipster kids
Psychedelic, Spanish music-making kids

"Keep expressing yourselves."

NICK ROSSI

YOUR YOUNG
SONG FADES STILL

your Saturn spits
gravel
    filling the ditches and mouths of
    crows
        lining the fields today,
        Saturday,
           garage sale sabbath. at dawn,
we are young and volatile, entangled
    in rubber cords, Pizza4U boxes, and
    greasy
        knots of hair. our voices
        cackle light
           over popping basslines, discount
freedom song from speakers blown and crackling,
    lifting up in spite of our work-stiff
    hands
        and backs. black coffee
        soothes, so
           the dull pain in our heads and
stomachs fades out onto empty side streets
    of this, our suburb. your
    future
        death cannot touch us
        here
           yet. these roads are not haunted
for us, still we speed as if escaping.

Neptune, color pencil on toned paper, by Anthonyxyz

STEELE

TO EAT THE FRUIT, CLIMB THE TREE

Of course I want
to sit with you—
to float weightless on your breath
above the bluebell and
the whitethorn
at the east end of the orchard.

Of course I want
to rest.

I want to sleep.
But listen,

we cannot let the landlords live.

STEELE

PARA COMER LA FRUTA, HAY QUE TREPAR EL ÁRBOL

Por supuesto que quiero
estar a tu lado—
flotar sin peso en tu respiro
por encima de las gardenias y
los rosales
al otro lado de tu jardín.

Por supuesto que quiero
descansar.

Quiero dormir.
Pero mira,

no podemos dejar que los dueños de apartamentos vivan.

(Translated by Nikolai Garcia)

CAROLINA BLANCHARD

CONTANDO MIL ESTRELLAS

Ando perdida

En el tiempo y el espacio

Detrás de tu despedida

Aún viviendo esa noche

Donde conté todas las estrellas

Brillando en tus ojos

CLAIRE KOOYMAN

AMOK

while I drove home,
following the speed limit and
wiping my eyes at lights
I thought
no one on this highway loves me,
fascinated,
surrounded by thousands of people,
no one cares
what happens
to me, the highway is one long
stretch of capitalism run amok,
and every employee in every store
would wish you a nice day,
but none would mean it.

KEVIN RIDGEWAY

THE DAY I TURNED INTO A MAN

My father had finally come home
after twelve years in a federal penitentiary.
It was the first birthday I spent with both
of my parents. The day I became
a teenager. My brother had moved
out of the house three months before,
so I had them both all to myself.
We decided to visit Forest Lawn
in the hills overlooking
the movie studios, where
we paid our respects to
the dead movie stars
who I worshipped with
the hope that I would escape
from my lonely childhood,
at a time when
black and white ghosts
kept me company, and when
I discovered who my parents
pretended to be before
they both became ghosts who
watched me grow up in the dark
in search of them all, in a place
where daydreams go to die.

KEVIN RIDGEWAY

MIDNIGHT HUSTLE

the drug dealer screams at me:
this ain't no game, bitch—
I got a right mind to
whoop your ass
right here in the gutter
but I scream *fuck you homie!*
and run across the intersection,
threatening to call the police
which gets him to bark harder
and I yell *never mind,*
I won't call the police,
please don't kill me
while a tripped-out dude
dances five steps forward,
five steps back over and over again
in a broken dance in front of me
while he blasts his Walkman
full of old school jams over by
where VIP Records used to be,
all of it rich in music history,
but now it's a vacant strip mall
for white boys to run across
in search of other white boys
who ran from the same
hardened men who are
all mistaken when they claim
we owe them money from
previous drug deals none
of us can remember.

ANTHONY J. CASSARINO

GUATEMALAN-BLEND TO GO

momentary cups of coffee
quick walks on the beach
it is all right to stop by
but it is
heartless

> to take something
> that does not belong to you
> we are not a cheap cup picked up from 7-Eleven
> pitched before the real work begins

we are the hard harvests
back breaking
freshly ground
beans of daybreak.

> the clay man is made from
> clay our ancestors built with
> brick that lays suburban homes
> brick the red ones have bled for

mountains cry for our attention
we sip our beverages, hearing the cars rumble
the medium roast whiffs of sweet caramel
it tastes like a bitter cigarette
and it burns my damn hand.

"damn paper cup"
coffee spews across the dashboard
bugs fly into the windshield
i swerve back and forth to make it to work

mornings feel better
when i watch the robins flutter
in my backyard
near the red maple
when my coffee comes to a slow chug
the dog springs out for a morning jog
and my hardest task
is washing my coffee cup

ミスターピンタムロ / 2019

Patlani, graphite pencil on paper, by Mr. Pintamuro

XOCHITL-JULISA BERMEJO

MAMITA, WE'RE GOING TO GO ON AHEAD

For Claudia Patricia Gómez

Mamita, when I crossed the Río Bravo I promise
I walked brave. You would've been proud
to see your princesita pushing against current.
When feet reached the shore they ordered us
to hide. I did my best to make my body soft
like the bank, but it wasn't enough.
Only a mile in and minutes on the land,
border patrol shot me. Long grasses held my body,
and I thanked them for the kindness.
With my face half in blood and half in dirt,
I heard a woman screaming. She named me
chava, ruca, muchacha. I wanted to thank her too,
but the grasses wrapped around my ears
and sang me to sleep. Mamita, don't cry.
I've gone on ahead, and one day, we'll be reunited,
but my blood stays behind. Deep, dark parts of me
soak the soil. Stain their precious border.

RICK SMITH

ARDMORE AVENUE, 1967

It felt good to hear Rita
use her key to enter my apartment
where I lay in a pool of sweat,
where I hadn't eaten in 2 days.

It felt good when she pulled out a $20 bill
and said, let's go to the Thrifty-Mart
and get you some groceries.

It felt good walking those well-lit aisles
tossing packages into the cart.

It felt good to make a plate
of bread and salami
and take down a can of Brew 102.

And it felt good to lie down
on that junk store mattress,
watch her peel off her jeans,
and climb under the sheets.
The stomach full,
the radio on,
the roar of the Hollywood Freeway
like surf pounding outside the window.

I had everything
a man could possibly want.

LUIVETTE RESTO

A LETTER TO GUS, THE JUDGMENTAL CVS CLERK

Dear Gus,

I didn't need the extra look of judgment
or the five-page receipt when I bought my Plan B pill

Yes, I had sex.
No, I didn't use a condom.
Yes, I enjoyed it, and
yes, Gus, I will do it again and again and again.

I don't think male customers get the same discernment
when they buy the industrial pack of Trojans,
extra thin and lubricated for her pleasure.

I am tired of my body being examined and decided upon
by men who couldn't find a clitoris
even if Alexa, Siri, and Google joined forces in some GPS version
of Voltron.

So save your visual admonishments
for I am not your Latin Mary Magdalene
although I am sure I did shout God's name more than once.

You will not side-eye me for fulfilling my sexual desires,
expressing my sensuality, savoring the taste of a man's touch,
satisfying my fantasies one orgasm at a time,
loving my body under my own terms.

Sincerely,
An Unapologetic Woman

LINDA DOVE

IN THE MORNING, PEACOCKS

stain the trees
of the neighborhood
where they don't belong
to anyone, interlopers
from the Arboretum
down the street, or
refugees, depending on
whether you believe
in the right to stake
a claim for yourself
in this world or if you
are running from
the efforts of fences.
The birds are like ballroom
curtains, their colors
so unbelievable, velvet
and the wilder parts
of the ocean where the deep

is satisfied. They peck
at the lawns. They avoid
the dogs being walked
on leashes to avoid
jawing their candied necks,
which bob as they go
like blue arrows. Before
full light, they seem to be
metal because of the feather
shine and because they are
not the size of sparrows.
They plumb from roosts
in the pines, wings tented
open, all topaz dazzle
and green and eyes,
the way fate might drop,
seen, into your day.

WILLIAM JOEL

SONNET FOR AN ANGRY SKY

"Wise Man: One who sees the storm coming before the clouds appear."
—Elbert Hubbard

While sitting at a coffee shop, my mug
of Joe at hand, I lift my eyes and stare
outside. Dark clouds have come like quiet thugs,
to loose their torrents on our heads, to tear
apart this peaceful afternoon before
I've had the chance to taste its flavors, smell
the rich aroma, calming. What's in store
will surely pass but not until all hell
breaks loose, until the anger in the skies
has had its way, expelled its wrath, to leave
us with the day it interrupted, tried
to sabotage. And sitting here, I weave
this simple poem, to tell the clouds I'll still
be here no matter how you wield your will.

TRICIA LOPEZ

NAZAR FOR WHAT'S LEFT BEHIND

In Nicaragua, my tías dyed my hair back
to black to get rid of the Sandinista red.
The broken cathedral, kissed by an old earthquake,
watched the waves crash into the malecón.
There were volcanos, *un sueño*
que un dia, when I saw Cale Cale dancing.
My grandfather's name was a broken
street, not *calle*, but a word we used
when he salsaed in his lab coat,
the test tubes and needles waiting
for him to get back to blood.
Now he kneels with a priest. If I drape
myself in thorns and drown
in *Flor de Caña*, there would be
his light, the softest shirt.
Now my mother's green ring covers
the tan on my finger, and I can no longer feel
the heartbeat of those days.
I sit on my balcony and wait
for the city's doves to fly over.

SHORT FICTION

PLUM CAKE FOR CLOWNS

BY MONIQUE QUINTANA

I TELL EVERYONE I DON'T LIKE MY MOM'S BOYFRIEND. EVEN SHE DOESN'T like him. She calls him a leech, she says he's a trick. That's what Manuel is: a circus clown, a trick, he does magic tricks for a living, for little kids at their birthday parties. My least favorite days are the ones where my mother calls me in her room to tell me something and she has her blankets up over her naked shoulders, like she's trying to be modest, like I can't smell Manuel on her. She thinks I can't see him outside her bedroom window, picking plums from our tree.

That's our tree! I tell him. I hold my apron out so he can throw the plums in there. Plums have a yearlong bruise just like we have a yearlong tan, he tells me. He's got his white face paint caked under his nails. He needs more ingredients for his plum cake, and my mother offers to go to the store and I know why.

She blow-dries her hair and teases it big. Puts a lot of eyeliner under her eyes and so much blush on her cheeks that it could rival Manuel's clown face. When we get to the store, she buys me a bear-shaped lemon cookie if I promise to clean my room when I get home. My dresses are thrown outside my room like they are corpses. She talks about corpses with the cashier kid. His dimples seem to glow on his face and I notice that he has grease stains on his khaki button-up shirt. I think about how good my mom would be at scrubbing those stains out for the kid. He tells my mom that he goes to the racetrack on Friday nights when he gets off work. The arcade at the racetrack has a karaoke night, he says, and I watch the way his hair swirls like an 'o' on top.

My mom and Manuel take me to the drive-in movies when the weather's nice outside. The other day his friend was working the ticket booth, so they waved us in for free. My mom's too cheap to buy stuff from the snack bar, so she brings a jug of iced tea and a paper grocery bag of popcorn she popped on the stove while humming the theme song from *Dark Shadows*. She tells me that Barnabas used to make her hide behind her television set when she was a kid. It's always hard to pay attention to the movie at the drive-in in our town. There's that racetrack next door and the cars roar and make our radios fuzz over what I think are the best parts of the movie. I think about that kid with dimples at the grocery store, the one that my mom always dresses up for. I hear my mom and Manuel's kiss smack when they think I'm asleep. The snack bar makes a pretty yellow glow across the lanes, and some boys I know from school sit next door to us in their fold-up chairs drinking from soda cans, long straws sticking out to the sky.

Manuel gets upset when we come home and we're missing something in our paper bags. He pulls out the containers of cream and the milk and the paper muffin cups and the cheap cherry lipstick my mom bought for me. Manuel pulls out the lipstick to see what color it is and it swivels until it gets cut off like a head. My mother yells at him for this and he yells back at her for forgetting the most important thing, the powdered sugar. I think powdered sugar tastes like chalk. *Why didn't you remember to get the pow-dered sugar?* Manuel asks me. I imagined him dusting the powder sugar all over his face. Ask her, I say and point to my mother. She was too busy talking to the cashier guy and she forgot to get it.

That was yesterday and Manuel sits outside with his plum cake, the eggs folded in, the tree shading his dark arms, dark stubble underneath the bits of scrubbed-off face paint. My mother clanks the breakfast dishes in the sink, her ankles shifting, her bright red shoes untied at the laces. The cake is sweeter than I thought it would be, even without the sugar. •

THE FURNACE
BY ROBERTO DÍAZ

"In the end, Karma reigns supreme." -Xerxes the Thunderbird

March 9th, 2015
Koreatown, Los Angeles, California
7:30 A.M., 44 Degrees Fahrenheit

SANTOS TOMAS NUÑEZ WAS TIRED OF BEING BLAMED FOR THE BAD LUCK at HiLo (Hispanic Legal Organization). He knew his tough decisions made him no friends, but rumors about him being a snake creature were untrue. It annoyed him to hear people say he was responsible for someone's death and the disappearance of another employee.

It must be because I'm a ginger, these people hate gingers, he told himself, downing a bottle of scotch in the elevator. His face had been broken in several places by a plaque the deceased underling threw at him while Santos tried out his cobra head costume for Halloween. He wore cufflinks engraved with the initials S.T.N., a reminder of life before the incident, when he enjoyed berating employees and colleagues. Now he stuck to phone calls.

Santos hated cold weather, as it hurt his joints. He thought of that when he fired the maintenance crew for failing to fix the boiler.

He laughed, thinking about how a highly trained lawyer was fixing their mistakes. Being a man of routine, he brought all the tools he needed and a brick to keep the door open in the boiler room. Sweat dripped down his slicked back hair when he realized he'd left his cell phone on his desk. *I'm almost done, I'm sure these idiots can handle five minutes unsupervised*, he mumbled to himself.

As he finished replacing the heating elements the lights flickered and he fell back, landing on his butt. He stood up and knocked the brick away, he turned around to catch the door but it was too late. *Fuck me, I'm stuck here.* He knocked on the door but nobody came. *Calm down, someone will come.*

He lit his last Natural American Spirit cigarette only to drop it seconds later after reading: Warning Fire Risk. The meticulous man had made a mistake, he watched as his lit cigarette landed on the uncovered circuit breaker and sparks flew. He rushed the door, hoping to save himself.

Santos Tomas Nunez told himself he wasn't a monster, he told himself he was a good man, he told himself he was just doing his job. The flames disagreed, and on that cold spring morning they devoured him. ·

CIRCLES AT HIGH NOON
BY HAOLUN XU

A SINGLE PHOTOGRAPH STOOD OUT ON A WALL. MARCUS LANGE, AT THE peak of his twenties, dressed in the full gear of a cowboy. His muscular body was in midair, jumping over a completely calm horse. Marcus had with him a lasso, fully cast out into a circle, with him framed in the middle of the rope. A very impressive acrobatic feat, the three dark shapes held in place against a cloudy sky. The man's face was downward and completely engrossed in the motion. Whoever looked at it could barely make out the facial expression, but the body showed a powerful sense of focus. The self-given title was written in faded black marker at the bottom of the frame.

"SOLAR ECLIPSE, 1990."

Connor, Marcus's nephew, sat in the kitchen in the present. He'd been staring at this picture for a while. He had admired the photo for years, it'd even been passed around for a while at a Thanksgiving just a few years back. There was something off about the picture. He remembered asking his uncle a few times if the horse was fake. He'd always gotten a laugh back. "No, no. That horse is real. Trust me, I smelled like horse all week after that."

It wasn't too friendly a visit. Connor came as a herald for the end times. His mother, Marcus's sister, wanted him to come back to Pennsylvania. Philadelphia, to be exact. There was no particular emergency, but with his father moving the paternal grandparents back to the Northeast, his mother felt similarly about bringing family closer into a cluster. She was worried about her brother, the truth of the matter was that the ranch had become too expensive to support alongside the other financial decisions going on. The family was getting bigger, cousins were getting married and children were being born or growing into expensive college students not unlike Connor.

But it wasn't as if she had sent him. Connor had volunteered, tired of the endless lectures at the University of Pittsburgh. He was fond of Marcus's stories, he was hardly a farmer or a rancher. His uncle had graduated from Boston University thirty years ago, specializing in physics and civil engineering. The time he had spent afterwards was largely abroad, working in odd and seemingly delightful areas such as Amsterdam and Germany. When Connor was a child, he would always get European chocolates as a gift. Marcus would come home every year for the holidays for a single night or two, before retreating to the same ranch.

There came a boom from the side of the house. Connor jumped, his back twisting towards the source of the noise. "What was that?"

Marcus came out, his face calm, with a bag filled with peanuts. The plastic was thin and transparent.

"Ah, she's awake. One of the mares from the farm two miles away. I'm keeping her close with me this week. She's been thrashing." He wiped his face with a hot towel from the sink. "She's lost her senses."

"The groundskeeper's coming tomorrow. I can afford a little bit there, and I know his cousin from the grocery store," he explained.

Connor sat alert, his back arched. He looked concerned towards his uncle. "What happened?"

Marcus sat down, the kitchen light shining on his forehead. His hairline had receded a bit the past two years.

"She had a foal a few months ago. It passed away from a fever during the spring. She hasn't adjusted to the loss well at all. No sleep, sometimes she forgets to eat. If you don't eat—that's one thing. But she forgets. She waits outside her door even though the food's right there. I don't think she'll be able to make it much longer after all this. It's been a harsh summer for her."

His uncle said this evenly, his voice steady as he said this. Connor blinked in surprise, unable to respond confidently to the story.

"Oh, that's terrible."

"It was tough. I haven't seen anything like that in a while. She's been lunging and rolling about. I found her a few days before you came on the ground, covered in mud. It was late at night, probably around two a.m. I tried to call out to her, I said, 'Clementine! Clementine!' I don't think she heard me. It was very upsetting. Maybe she didn't care, I don't even know if she knew it was raining."

He added a little bit more, softly. "It's raining tonight too."

Connor nodded, taking out a peanut. "Is there anyone else coming?"

A grunt. "There's Corey, he's a little older than you. Quirky kid, he came in from California to get away from school."

Connor breathed in slowly and proceeded with hesitation. "Mom asked if you're seeing anyone out here. She asked me if you were going on any cute movie dates, here in-" he gestured with his arms, "-farm country."

"No, there's no one out here for me but good friends," he replied. He laughed, his eyes folding from the smile.

Brussel sprouts lay in a dish nearby, coated in dark sauce, laden with cold grease. The taste of freedom. Cartoon hardiness. A small garage-sale lamp held its own position atop the wooden table. Connor thought to himself, at least a marriage would be good for his uncle. The married life, there would be some life at all. Instead, he watched as the paint peeled quickly off the walls, the paper chipping away rather quickly.

"I think that's fair," Connor chose his words carefully. "There's not many people out here in the countryside."

The pained noises of the horse started again. There was an awkward emptiness in the air as they paused to listen.

"You don't get lonely?" Connor asked.

"And to be like that?" His uncle drew his head back, motioning to the stables. "To be like that." He repeated, shaking his head. His eyes turning to the floor as he did this.

Sounds came abruptly, as if the horse was in great physical pain. The two quietly fed themselves with the growing pile of shells and nuts on the table.

* * *

"Can we set up a small fence? Something made of steel. Just to scare her off the distance." Corey squinted as he said this. He was physically smaller than Connor. When the two shook hands earlier, Corey made two jokes about size.

"None, she runs over across each of the bounds," the groundskeeper said. The groundskeeper had a placid stare. His tall body stood against the wind. It was this temperament that a lack of personality, limited flair, and a fatigue that could be easily mistaken for calm. But it wasn't calm, it wasn't much at all.

The mare had broken out of the stables earlier in the week, taking down several gates of yellow pine. It was now clear it would take more than two proxies to bring her back into shelter. The figure of the horse had been elongated by the morning sun earlier, but in the light of day, the interrupted and disjointed rhythm of its gallop became painstakingly clear. Even Corey knew that by the end of the weekend, if they had not gotten to her, she would do herself in. The muscles, slamming against the ground, could be seen ripping painfully as she thrashed.

"It's a very difficult fight," the groundskeeper continued. "It's hardly worth punishment for any of us."

Even with the words, there was a hint of unpredictability to the whole ordeal. They watched, trying not to shift their weight, staring into the distance.

"Does one of us really have to go get her?" Corey asked. He laughed, then stopped. He had heard her crying out into the daylight. Her breath could almost be seen, like steam being blasted from a train. He visualized bringing her in. Corey's family housed a small barn across town, with a single emergency space now for the mare.

Marcus hoisted a tied lasso onto his shoulder, made from thick yellow rope. It didn't seem heavy at all to him, despite the length making up a substantial weight. Connor thought about how he had carried it for a few minutes as Marcus put on his boots.

"It's the same weight as a gun. It's always surprising, it seems much lighter," Connor had noted.

"A lasso is important. It needs to have that balance, between the man holding it and the tension and the counterweight." Marcus had said. "There's this idea that horses would have become extinct in North America if humans hadn't domesticated them. The ancestors of horses, equi, became as extinct as mammoths during the Ice Ages. Something like that."

The groundskeeper checked the rope as he surveyed Marcus's face. There was something tense about him. "I can call Browning from A.C. He can fix this for you, and you could simply watch."

"No, no. This is my ranch, and you know I love that horse. I told you this."

Marcus had grown attached to the mare. He'd spent some time on the main horse ranch earlier in June, and watched as the groundskeeper had nursed the foal with medicinal water and ice packs. It was a painful ordeal, and they didn't mention how much the foal smelled like a newborn, wet with fresh hay and soft love. When the foal passed, they had cremated him far away from the mare, but she had sensed the burning anyways. Corey had been watching over her as she whinnied, the loss accounted for even though they made sure to drive the foal's body several miles away. He stared ahead. It was just a wide-open space, and on that day a lone horse, stampeding herself into further grief.

"Alright, here she comes, boys." Marcus said. "Connor, stay in the back. She runs faster than you'd think."

His uncle was right. When the mare started to circle closer and closer to the group, Connor noted how large she was. It felt like an entire brown hill had arrived in front of him, moving back and forth like a mobile volcano. The cries were filled with fury, and Connor instinctively drew up his hands. Even the wind she carried on her back, built on her speed, could be felt as she came closer.

They realized she could barely recognize them. Her head was swaying back and forth, caught between a nightmare and the wake of day. There was no time for hesitation now, only whatever gentleness they could muster. The sun cast a light against their eyes, despite the cloudy mix in the sky.

"Easy! Easy!" The groundskeeper and Corey began to loop around her at a wide distance, countering her spin with their own. She didn't slow down, simply rampaging into the wet earth as her movement continued. Her son, her son. But she knew where her foal had gone, and she would have no recourse until the rage subsided and the next began.

She started to run towards Corey, and he flashed his own lasso towards her. She drew herself up, the front legs pumping into the air as she did this. Corey saw the full height of the mare and yelled out in fright.

"Ahhh! Marcus, do it! Do it now!"

Marcus ran forward, the lasso started to spin as he drew

the rhythm of the rope forward. He skipped his feet, one-two in timing with the mare. He saw only the flash of her brown body, the hoofs jutting out against his own body. He let out a roar and flung the rope towards her.

Marcus now must've been nervous. He tried to calm his teeth from chattering, and he forced back memories of Berlin and Vienna. For an instant, he lost his sight completely. He thought only about his young nephew behind him, the eyes watching his body as he disappeared into the small storm in front of him. Time was lost, for a moment, and he felt strangely connected with his men. But the harmony fell out with the rope, and he lost sight of her. In an instant, she broke away, the rope slashing into her ear before being thrown off into the side.

The mare stormed forward, shrieking out in confusion. This wasn't the first time this week that she'd been contained, but this time was different. There was something painful in the air, there were too many bodies present and it broke her heart. She smashed into the earth with her hoofs and each step she took became stronger.

Perhaps she recognized Marcus, somewhere between how he stood and the way he tried to call out to her. This might've saved his life, but nevertheless she tackled him the second he tried to fling his body out of the way. There was a half-cry from both man and horse, and the uncle was knocked onto the mud.

This time Corey, the groundskeeper, and Connor ran over to the man. He was bleeding out of his nose and breathing through an open and shocked mouth. Connor was frightened, he'd never seen his uncle bleed, he didn't know if he'd ever seen his family bleed before.

Corey yelled out, "She's running off!" The mare had in fact fled, her figure now several meters away in full gallop into the high sun. She made new sounds this time, fear and betrayal and frustration as the steam of her breath rose off her vanishing frame.

The groundskeeper took out his cell phone. "I'll call Browning from Animal Control. I told him last night, if worse comes to worst, he'll take up after her. We have a wild horse now, she wasn't wild before but now she's gone and done it."

The man went rushing off into the house, as Connor held his uncle in his arms. Marcus held onto his nephew's shirt, clinging onto it with mud all over his hands. "It's just my time-" he managed to speak out.

Corey watched, pleading with the man with empty noise. "Please! Mr. Lange! It's okay! You broke some ribs! It'll be alright."

The uncle gasped for air. He tried his best to stay calm, but adrenaline had made its way fully to his mind. He gestured weakly and abruptly at the ground, he wanted to stay put, he didn't want to move. The grass, trampled and split, clung to his arms and neck. They felt like fire, rendering his entire skin into different textures of pain.

The nephew held onto his uncle's dirty hands as they trembled fanatically. He looked his uncle straight in the eyes, both pairs desperate and luminously alert.

"That's enough," the nephew sputtered out. His eyes were completely trained on his uncle. "That's enough."

The uncle gasped, each breath more livid than the last. This was his answer, as he tried his best not to cry in front of the young men, his lungs caught between disorder and heartbreak. Despite the silence around them, the ringing in their ears sang out.

"That's enough. Please, please."

The old man shut his eyes, his body numb from the shock. All he felt was his hands gripped so tightly in another's, his heart pounding so hard it went far, far into the plains with the mare. •

THE CARVERIANS 2

BY SONDRIAWRITES

Excerpt from the forthcoming short story collection series

(Illustration by Darya Farhoodi)

MANGGIH SAT LOCKED IN HER OFFICE FOR THE SEVENTY-SECOND HOUR WITH her large hands pressed into her desk, analyzing her relationship with Panyadia (called Yadi) and Papayung. She cross-referenced her words with her actions, and finding no discrepancies by the seventy-third hour, she allowed a rage older than herself to engulf her.

The Rage pummeled through and replaced the blood cells in Manggih's ears making them hot with condescending laughter at the idea that she could either allow or disallow it. She wrapped her arms tightly around her breasts, rocked front to back, and cracked her stiffened-straight fingers into cups around her elbows. She breathed hollowly and stared blankly while The Rage gossiped with itself on either side of her mind.

"Little girl talmbout she *allowed* me," the rage in the right hemisphere poked.

"Allowed *us!*" The rage in the left hemisphere prodded. And the two laughed angrily and slapped hands creating an electrical current in the longitudinal fissure that separated them.

Manggih's eyes stared on, unmoved and stubbornly dry from the doctor's demonstration of her ability to control the so-called involuntary act of blinking. Her fingernails dug deeply into the fatty flesh about her elbows, anchoring against her subconscious fear that they may spring back into stiffened straightness. Synapses exploded all over Maggih's brain, drowning out The Rage. The rage in the left hemisphere cut its eyes at the streams of thick, purple liquid rolling from the doctor's elbows and landing in disappearing drops on the soil surrounding her desk.

"All *I'm* saying is," The Rage sounded faint as the last synapse in Manggih's brain burst. "If the bitch can't control her own fingers, she may as well blink." The doctor's arms fell dead at her sides, then the bitch blinked.

When Manggih's eyes opened again, her sclera was jet black and the pupils were a tiny, glowing light. The light grew rapidly, then burst through Manggih's eyelids in a powerful beam that thrust her head back. Lava-colored twin-pupil beams sliced, like a laser, through the three-foot-thick ceiling made of interwoven ivy roses. The plant's severed limbs squirmed on the floor before dying. They were scorched to cremation by the overzealous sunlight that shone enthusiastically, overcompensating for generations of being shut out. "Yes..." Manggih said faintly... I understand."

The doctor was in a trance, reliving her past. Her body was contorted about the neck and her eyes were shooting luminance. Seventy-five hours ago she had stormed into her office to think.

"If I am disturbed, the consequences will be devastating," Manggih told the ivy roses. They crawled the walls, slithered the floors, and creeped the ceilings happily spreading the new law. But instead of retiring to her many isolation caves, the doctor walked into her Open-door Policy office, leaving the door open behind her. She placed both her hands flat on her desk and lowered herself slowly into her chair, still dazed by the dual betrayal she had just witnessed.

Seventy-seven hours ago Manggih and her horses were in a mossy marsh covered in green mud practicing synchronized yoga. They were under the tutelage of the thick fog hovering above the marsh at about Manggih's height. The fog, which was also green, camouflaged the practitioners. Even the ivy roses had to skulk around surrounding areas panicked at not being able to locate their obsession by her scent beyond the green mud. And that was the doctor's intention—a trick she had learned as a rebellious teenager.

All at once, the ivy roses stopped moving. They waited for proof that what they thought they had just felt was real. Accepting the second vibration as confirmation, the wandering plant reunited, unsheathed its shiny, metal thorns, and burrowed underground to discreetly seek out the source.

The ivy roses didn't always have metal thorns. And they weren't always so vicious, jealous, and controlling. Back when they were young, before they had met Manggih's father–the black man that talked to plants–their thorns were short, green, and soft. They were used more like *feelers*, and they were as sensitive to the touch as nipples.

That was before their genocide. Back when sweethearts used to clip their buds from time to time, and exchange their carcasses as symbols of appreciation for one another. The spirits of the ivy roses that hovered in the homes of young lovers for eternity were at peace. It was Valentine's Day that hardened them. A few buds lost at the fingers of well-intentioned kids was no threat at all. But the miles of flesh harvested by big-business machinery for no one in particular, (but *anyone* from which they could manipulate money) was devastating. The ivy's blood boiled with rage, melting off the soft green feelers and replacing them with sharp, shiny weapons. The new thorns were a match for the machines, and the way the plant learned to slither, crawl, burrow, and creep, kept them out of human reach.

After a while of being headed in its direction, the ivy roses had come to the source of the vibration, and stopped at a distance to observe. A tiny, glowing seed sprang glowing, tiny roots. The tiny, glowing roots became thick and strong before breaking through the surface of the soil as a glowing bark. Glowing branches sprang from the head of the glowing bark, then hung heavy with the weight of the glowing flowers, glowing leaves and glowing fruit that appeared as well.

Above the ground, Yadi plucked a glowing piece of fruit from the glowing tree and took a bite. The ivy roses hissed. Then the glowing tree swallowed Yadi in its lush branches and snatched him underground. The ivy roses started to rescue him until they noticed the lackadaisical pleasure on his face as he ate of the glowing tree fruit. Yadi didn't need rescuing. He was home. The heartbroken ivy watched as the tree pulled Yadi further and further away until it was just a tiny, pupil-sized glow.

There was a second vibration approaching. This one from above ground. The ivy quieted. Papayung stopped running where he thought he'd seen Yadi enter the forest and where Manggih and her horses had just seen the flash of light, but he saw nothing. The ivy roses watched him from below as he spun around and paced trying to find evidence of his old friend. Manggih watched from a distance—rage gently playing her eardrums like a timpani. Papayung emerged from the place Yadi had disappeared and started running back toward Carveria. The ivy roses swam below him, speeding, to relay this information of glowing roots and secret fruits and Yadi's truth to Manggih, who had thought she'd seen all she needed to see—her lovers with their own secrets.

The doctor and her chariot of horses were the first of the observers to reach Carveria and when she got there she demanded no one disturb her, no exception. That had been twenty-three hours ago. Manggih's fingertips were now pressing hard into the desk as she replayed what she'd seen from the foggy marsh over and over. She was dehydrated. Her lips were dry and starting to crack. Two plant valet's entered her office with water having felt her deficiency through their biological connection. They bowed before her, offering up the chilled pitcher and glass. Manggih heard some faint laughter echoing her mind and unsheathed the knife from her thigh holster. She sliced one valet at the belly and it split in half. The glass landed softly on the soil. Then the doctor sliced the second valet's throat, knocking the pitcher to the ground.

"KEEP FUCKING PLAYING WITH ME!" She screamed and allowed her dry lips to split and bleed, reholstering her weapon. Then she sat back down and replaced her hands to keep thinking about her lovers over the years. The background laughter in her mind was getting louder and louder. She stared blankly ahead.

"Do you see now?" The Rage asked Manggih with lava beams shooting from her eyes.

"Yes," Manggih answered languidly. "I understand." •

PRE-ORDER THE CARVERIANS 2 ON 9/15
GO TO SONDRIAWRITES.LIFE

NONFICTION

Digital Collage by Giana De Dier

HERMANA, TU NOMBRE LO LLEVO GRABADO

(SISTER, I HAVE SAVED YOUR NAME)

BY JENISE MILLER

Memoir Essay

I LANDED IN PANAMA'S TOCUMEN INTERNATIONAL AIRPORT, NOT SURE I would recognize my sister's face. She was fourteen years older than me and we had only met and learned about each other three years earlier. That year, Panama celebrated one hundred years of independence and Panamanians who lived abroad journeyed back to the beloved country they had not seen in decades. For my parents, it meant reuniting with distant relatives and loved ones, hair full of "las hojas blancas" El Gran Combo and Rubén Blades sang about. For me, it meant visiting their home country for the first time and meeting the sister and brother I didn't know I had. It felt strange, being introduced as adults, by our father who left Panama and didn't return for thirty years. That short meeting would be the only time I saw them.

This time, I journeyed back alone. I was in graduate school and asked my father to ask my sister if I could stay with her during spring break. They had grown close and talked frequently since that first trip. I used my financial aid to buy a last-minute ticket, a red-eye flight from LAX that flew six and a half hours, across Central America. I recognized her immediately. Out of all our siblings, she resembled our father the most. The shiny black waves that curved her face when we first met were now bright, honey blonde flecked with deep brown. The color brought out the dark reddish-brown skin that would label her chola in Panama and red-boned in the States. I don't recall if there were hugs when I arrived at the gate, though I'm sure there was the common courtesy of a kiss on each cheek. With a banal look she said, "*Well, let's go*," before directing me out of the airport.

She drove a black compact car that had the bounce and roar of an old stick shift. She hopped onto the highway, the thick grey smog and tropical humidity clouding the sky. The car-to-car traffic mimicked freeways back home in Los Angeles, "tranque," she called it, with smaller cars than the usual mix of SUVs, trucks, and even Hummers on the 110 freeway. The first time I saw a Toyota Yaris was in Panama, driven by a tall man whose knees sat in his chest as he drove it. She lived in a barriada in Panama City close to the airport. On the way to her house, she pointed out El Machetazo, the superstore where she worked.

At her house, she opened the suitcase my aunt in L.A., *our aunt*, sent with me: lovingly packed clothes and accessories from

Ross for her and her two adult daughters. She tried on a white jean jacket then dumped it on the clothes piled atop the suitcase. She got up, left the clothes on the floor, and said in Spanish, the only language she spoke and I mostly understood, "I won't be cooking while you're here. There's no man here, no reason to cook or clean." She pointed out the microwave, microonda, the first word of many I would learn from my oldest sister, a woman I was now seeing for only the second time in my life.

Someone banged on the gate. She swung it open and spoke intensely to the person on the other side. As I sat on the couch, the conversation became louder, like an argument, with the baritone voice I could not see. One of her daughters, launched into the room, stood by her mother's side, fiercely protective. The conversation ended and she closed the door.

She paused for a moment then came over to where I sat on the couch pretending to be invisible. She said that the man at the door was her soon-to-be ex-husband and explained how they came to be separated. I was surprised that she would share details with me, someone she knew for less than 48 hours. An incident like this back home would have remained unexplained and understood as none of my business. My mother implored us never to share personal business with anyone outside of the family, a lesson she lived. My sister and I were acquainted, but not forged by years, secrets, and hurts that often seemed the proof of familial love. She did not turn her anger or hurt away from me, this stranger she just picked up from the airport, nor changed the subject. She shared and explained what I just witnessed, with an openness I had not experienced in my family.

That night, I slept in her bed while she roomed with one of her daughters. I stayed up in the silent dark, interrupted by the call of crickets and mosquitoes, heat and humidity, thinking about how far I was from home.

The next morning, she informed me that the showers in her house were not the steamy, warm showers I was used to at home. Her warning did not prepare me for the icy shower stream that shocked me and removed all weariness from the night before. Her daughters worked and attended college and would not get home until late in the day. My vacation was not their vacation. After I got dressed, I went into the bathroom to fix my hair. She came in and asked if I had any eyeliner. I looked through my bag and pulled out a black eyeliner pencil.

"This is the only color you have?!" she asked.

"Yes," I said, as confused as she was.

"Just black?!" She said, "No other colors? No brown, no purple?" She said "purpura," a word I was not familiar with. I knew "morado." Purpura, she explained, was the deep purple that complemented brown skin; morado was light purple, closer to lavender. I did not have purpura or morado eyeliner and, until that moment, had not considered that I should line my eyes in any other color.

I accompanied her to work for a short shift that morning. Before she left me in the makeup section (perhaps, a hint that I should explore the colored eyeliner), she explained, "The stores here in Panama are not like the stores in the States, where you can just open up the nail polish in the store and put it back after you've tried it." She left. As I looked at the nail polishes, I noticed a clerk eyeing me...

My sister found me in the aisles at the end of her shift. "Do you like soup?"

We headed to a local mall and stopped first at a food counter that served all kinds of soups and stews. We agreed we both loved soup so much, we could eat it on the hottest day. My mother made chicken soup with yucca, plantain, corn on the cob, and dumplings, which I presumed was the type of soup offered here. I asked her if she knew which one of the soups had dumplings. "Oh, you know about dumplin?" she laughed. "We call that 'chombo'* soup. They don't sell that here, that's the kind of soup you make at home."

*The Panamanian equivalent to the N-word, in its racist origin, used by whites in Panama against Black, often West Indian-descended, Panamanians, and in its current form, as a term embraced by some Black Panamanians while still seen as offensive by others, and still activated by whites as an insult.

The chicken soup was delicious, though not as good as my mother's. From there, we walked store to store, as I looked for souvenirs for my mother, nieces, and nephews back home. I told her I hated shopping; it conjured up the anxiety of growing up with every check-out a tense negotiation of items to remove or leave altogether because the money was short. She said the mall could be pricey, so we left for a street lined with small shops. We entered a clothes store. As she perused airy dresses and blouses, she said "You go to the store before you get paid. You see what you like and if it's still here when you return, it was meant for you." She enjoyed it, taking the time to coordinate separate pieces, the reward of finding good deals; a departure from the stress I felt with the task.

In my last-minute preparation for the trip, I did not have time to get a protective style that would have saved me the daily question of what to do with my hair. My sister explained that she styled her hair with a blower:

"They straighten the hair with a brush and a [high heat] blow dryer."

"A brush?!" I laughed, "No, my hair needs something stronger than that. Like a hot comb. Do you have one?" My Spanish failed me, I did not know how to translate hot comb or flat iron. "A comb made of iron that you put on the stove," I said.

"Ahh!" she exclaimed, this Spanish version of "ohhh," but more confident and dramatic. "My grandmother used one of those." Exactly, I needed the old school tools. She did not have one.

I wanted to ask if there was a local salon where I could get my hair braided, since Panama City had a large population of Black Panamanians. I braided a section of my hair to show her the style I did not have the name for. "Moños," she said [though braids are more popular now, the common word is trenzas]. "I think our aunt does braids."

"Who?" I asked, only familiar with our aunts in L.A.

"Our aunt, the youngest daughter of our grandfather."

Our grandfather had two older sons, with our father being the eldest. Years later, she explained, he had another son and daughter, our father's half-brother and -sister. She knew this younger aunt and uncle, as well as the grandfather I never met. She knew and had relationships with the family that lived and remained in Panama, while I knew the family that came to the States. If we were all in the same place, what kind of family would we have been? We were all related and how we related to each other depended on which part of the world we lived.

As she took me to see the Panama Canal, Panama Viejo, and other historical sites, we talked family history and heartbreak. She pointed out where our grandfather once lived. She told me our grandmother remarried him after her second husband died. She grew up with him in her life, while I grew up with our father in mine. She told me about her mother, who had passed away years before, that she walked around the house with her hands always cold and my sister did not realize she was dying. Every day with her was a new place, a new word, a new bridge that connected my understanding of a family that lived miles and countries apart.

As my trip ended, I wanted to check-in for my flight online. She did not have a computer with Internet at home so she took me to a local Internet café. She asked me about setting up an email account. I set up an email and instant messenger account for her with a quick tutorial on using both. After I returned home, we communicated via messenger. She sent me one email:

"UN FAVOR TUYO TU PUEDES INTERPRETARME UNOS MENSAJES DE UNOS AMIGOS MIOS DE INTERNET QUE HABLAN INGLÉS... aprendido mucho en la computa grasias [sic] por todo tu clase fue corta pero efectiva que fue un entretenimiento para mi." Red Rose emoji. "Chao."

* * *

Later that year, our grandmother in California passed away. My sister traveled to L.A. for the first time in her life. She wore a black and white sheath dress to the funeral, with a matching sun hat that slightly veiled her eyes. She did not hesitate to stand and share her love and experiences with our grandmother, which made it clear to me, that despite being in different countries, she maintained a relationship with her I did not have.

At the repast, she told me I made her look crazy when she explained to our cousins that I spoke Spanish. When one cousin said, "She doesn't speak Spanish," my sister replied, "I don't speak English, how else do you think we talk?" In that moment, I could not prove the cousin wrong, could not open my mouth to parade the fluency my sister knew. She didn't know I could only speak Spanish with her. She did not get flustered when I spoke incorrect words or mismatched tense. She would gently say, you mean this or this or this and nod in approval at my corrections. I did not feel rejected or discouraged when I misspoke. There was space for my imperfection, for improvement. I discovered my ability to speak a new language, found comfort in that foreign place with her.

She remained in L.A. for several weeks and we both stayed with our aunt. I took her with me to work every day. From there, a male friend would pick her up and take her to tour the town - to Hollywood, the beach, to visit his mother in a nursing home. Of course, I sized the friend up and made sure I had his number. Apparently, he was an acquaintance of our father and hung out at a Panamanian-owned furniture shop with him. When our aunt questioned me about this, I said I did not know much about it. Once, my sister asked me to borrow a coat; coming from Panama's heat and humidity, she did not realize how cold it would be. I showed her a couple from the closet. What I thought meant coat was actually jacket, something light. She pulled out a white windbreaker that fit her perfectly. I only witnessed moments like this on TV—the instinct to defend, the sharing of clothes, as measures of sisterhood. For a moment we were sisters who lived in the same house, shared clothes, talked about love and loss in our family, looked out for each other. When it was time for her to return to Panama, my father and I saw her off at the airport.

* * *

She returned to L.A. three years later. During her brief trip, she stayed with our aunt and the two of them spent the days shopping for the upcoming wedding of her eldest daughter. I had recently moved into the first place of my own and she stopped by before catching her flight, with the promise to see each other later that year at the wedding in Panama. The other sister I grew up with on this side of the world, who I barely knew as a child because she was nine years older and barely knew as an adult because of her drug addiction, who was the only reference I had for a sister before my sister in Panama, was parked outside. My distant-but-close sister from Panama went outside and introduced herself to my close-but-distant sister from the States, even though that sister refused to come inside to meet her, even though that sister said "I only have one sister," when I told her our sister from Panama was here. In that instance, that sister showed herself to be the same person I knew her to be, and my sister from Panama showed herself to be the same person I had come to know. In that instance, I knew what it meant to have a sister by relation and a sister by relationship and that some distances grow too wide to cross.

* * *

Two months later, on the way home from a road trip with friends, we stopped to watch the Boston Celtics and L.A. Lakers NBA finals game. While my friends cheered the home team, I did not feel obligated to love a team just because it was located closest to me. I rooted for the Celtics—they ascended from being one of the worst teams to winning the championship, inspired partly by the brotherhood and mantra their coach emphasized: ubuntu – I am because we are. During the game, I received a phone call from my father's cousin, who was like an aunt to me. "I'm sorry to hear about your sister," I heard her say. The call was unusual – she lived in New York and we did not talk often. I had not received a call from my father or mother, which surely my mother would have called with urgency to inform me that something happened to my sister. I told her I was out of town and not sure what she meant. She said, "I'm sorry, I was mistaken, I'll talk to you later." We ended the call. The Celtics won that game but eventually lost it all.

When I arrived home, my mother told me my sister in Panama died. She had a stroke. For years, I didn't understand what happened, the facts of her death lost in translation. She was only 44 years old and had not been ill. It was years later that the same cousin-aunt explained that she had a brain aneurysm that she could not survive.

* * *

I knew my sister for seven years, not even enough time for our first disagreement. The memories I carried felt like a lifetime's worth. Yet, most of them fit within these pages. She had a name that I loved yet accidentally misspelled when I set up her email and messenger accounts. She forgave me. For months after she died, I would log onto the computer and see her name, dimmed and faded in the messenger box, just as I had saved it.

I didn't make the trip to Panama for the funeral. Through tears, I wrote a note at our aunt's house and asked her to read it there. It was in English; I did not have the words in Spanish for all I wanted to say and could not turn to my sister once more to cross the gap. I didn't feel like I had earned the grief, the sadness I felt, didn't deserve sympathy like those who were closest to her and had years worth of memories to mourn. Perhaps, I was accustomed to the physical distance, not needing to be close to feel close. We were sisters, despite the short time and long distance. We became sisters, because of it. •

THE STREETS ARE MADE OF ANGER
BY EVA RECINOS
South Central L.A. Memoir Essay

SOUTH CENTRAL LOS ANGELES MAKES YOU ONE OF TWO STATISTICS: YOU either made it out or you didn't.

There's no bench at the bus stop. Most days, my mom and I perch on a small edge of concrete landscaping that juts out from under the fence of the house behind us. We hold our bags on our laps, crane our necks to see if the bus is nearby. On weekends, we ride it to run errands—to the mall or church or the cemetery to drop off flowers for my dad.

Some evenings, when I'm already home, my mom calls our landline to ask me to meet her at the same stop, to help her carry the groceries home. It's one of those evenings when my cousin drags me out of the house. We pass the barking dogs next door, duck our heads under the heavy bougainvillea drooping over the neighbor's gate. We avoid the large cracks in the sidewalk, the fallen palm tree husks. He hardly talks. An ice cream truck passes by, which I recognize because of its refrain: a cheery "hello!" in between classic childhood songs.

The neighborhood feels calm and at ease. I know its duality by now: a familiar face that can turn dark.

I learn these things young. In my elementary school, the kids start passing around important bits of information, like how a pair of shoes hanging from an electrical cable means someone was killed on that block. Clothing is important, too—you need to avoid wearing red or blue, the hues of the warring gangs. The same goes for bandanas in those colors. We file these coded symbols away, a language we learn to speak early on. Our minds become repositories for basic math and for avoiding violence; we exchange info then go back to playing tetherball.

That evening, my cousin and I wait at the corner diagonal from the stop, looking for the orange of the bus approaching. I stand there oozing grief—for my dad, and for the more innocent time when the fear of losing people I love didn't even cross my mind. I long to get back to my room, where I can journal and play guitar badly.

Almost no one walks on our block, unless they live here. And you definitely don't walk around after dark, unless you're fearless. We feel safer inside the house, even while we can hear the cacophony of sirens, helicopter blades, yelling, and distant pops around us.

A group of people, mostly women, gather on the corner directly across from us, near the car wash. They're loud and energetic, seemingly excited about something. We don't pay them much attention at first. In our neighborhood, people often congregate outside their houses. They work on their trucks; water their lawns; sip on beers and let the empty ones clink down to the sidewalk.

But the group across the street gets louder, harder to ignore. Two or three people break off from the pack and walk in our direction. As they move slowly past us, one of them lets out a stream of spit that lands on the sidewalk near my feet. So close that I know it's not an accident. It's a challenge.

When I see her in my peripheral vision, the girl is not much taller than me but she stands out because she's so much younger than the rest of the group—much closer to my age. Neither of us looks old enough to buy cigarettes, but we're wizened enough to know the implications of this interaction.

I keep my gaze steady, looking forward. Maybe we exchange words, but my memory falters here. On the broken sidewalks of my neighborhood, two girls can fight on any corner—especially when the anger of their respective lives threatens to boil over. I'm furious at the swift truth that sometimes people die without warning; angry that I can't mend my mother's broken heart; resentful that our neighborhood holds such beauty but also so much danger. A certain anger seems to pulsate from the girl, too. We are two magnets with the same poles, bristling against each other.

At this age, I wear my anger like regalia: black clothing, black nails, chunky boots, thick wristlets with spikes on them. A chain wallet in one of my pant pockets. I crown myself as someone who knows the truth now, that life can be cruel. I model my look after the alt rock and punk bands I play on repeat. I leave behind my love for Jordans and thick shoelaces tied around my hair for something darker.

She tugs on the chain of my wallet. I realize she's poking fun at my effort to look tough. I turn to her and hiss.

"Ooh," the girl says, circling around me. "She hisses."

Suddenly, her arm hits the side of my neck. She keeps walking, as if she didn't even hit me in the first place.

Out of the corner of my eye, I see the bus has arrived. My mom crosses the street just as the girl gets closer to me. My mom tries to mediate the situation, to create some space between the two of us. The other women the girl crossed over with stand in the background and watch. My mom speaks to the girl, tries to calm her down.

"Shut up, you pussy-ass bitch," the girl says to her.

Everything boils over. My mom and I are hardly talking at this point—my dad's death caused a rift between us—but a line has been crossed. I know she's tired from work and weary from carrying her grief. I'm angry, too, and I hate that I have to steel myself against this interaction when I really just want to be home, in my room with my grief and no one to bother me.

"Don't call my mom a bitch!" I scream.

I lunge at the girl but my mom and cousin hold me back. I will myself forward, trying to wrench myself away from them and hurl myself towards her. Looking back, I can't remember if someone held the girl back, too. I can't remember how we end up walking away, but we do.

When we get home, my mom turns all three locks on our two front doors. An automatic movement I've also been taught to complete each evening. My body eventually stops shaking and I retreat to my room, the adrenaline slowly leaving my body as I sit against the headboard of my canopy bed, the one with white frilly sheets in a unicorn print. I feel older now, out of place.

Around this time, I dream that a man on the street threatens me in some way, just around the corner from our house. He tries to hurt my mom or family. I don't see the events unfold but I know this, in the strange way you hold knowledge in your dreams without explanation. I manage to get the upper hand in a struggle with him and I grab him by the hair. It's just long enough for me to wrap my fingers around it and get a really good grip. He's lying on the sidewalk suddenly, unable to get up.

I slam his head repeatedly into the sidewalk.

He tried to hurt me.

He tried to hurt my family.

He can't get away with it.

When I wake up, this unbridled violence scares me. Would that spark actually turn into a flame in a moment of danger? Am I just looking for an excuse to let out something darker?

I wonder how I got him on the ground. Why I couldn't stop

bashing his head into the concrete.

That evening at the bus stop, my mom and cousin kept me from releasing this rage into violence. This girl was right in front of me, and I was practically begging her to give me reprieve from the loud thoughts in my head. Part of me, lusting, for our fists to sort it all out.

After I leave my childhood neighborhood for graduate school—and even after I return to L.A. but live in a string of different neighborhoods—she often comes to my mind.

I wonder what went through her head, what she wanted, what she needed. I wonder if they groomed her, precisely for this moment. A rite of passage, an initiation. I could've been on the corner with that group, too. The same neighborhood, just a short walk away from her, but worlds away. I wonder who she's lost, who hurt her, who promised her protection and affection and gave it to her in all the wrong ways. I want to know if when she crossed back to the other side of the block, and rejoined the group on the corner, they congratulated her and she felt accomplished, proud.

We were so close in age. She couldn't have lived that far from me. We could've been friends, sat next to each other in class, chatting over the soundtrack of our nearby crushes rapping their knuckles rhythmically against the tops of their desks. We could've shared all the ways the city and the people in our lives broke our heart. How we loved our neighborhood but not the men who leered at us.

How we soaked in the sun on weekends but were only allowed to ride our bikes to the end of the block and back. How we marveled at kids from other parts of the city: the multiple parks and grocery stores walking distance from their homes; the undisturbed silence in their neighborhoods at night; their swimming pools and multiple bathrooms; the way they only worried about homework and chores, never about violence.

The headlines and thinly veiled comments from people outside of our block would paint us as two girls in a rough part of town—no manners, no guidance, no real future. No chance of making it out. People only pass through this part of the city. Reporters get back in their news vans, and we stay behind.

As I got older, I started dreaming of leaving my neighborhood—of buying my mom a bigger house in a quiet area of the city. But my heart also broke a little at the thought; this was the only home I knew. I entered its threshold as a newborn and slammed its doors as a pre-teen. The rooms still had imprints of my father's presence; I couldn't imagine leaving it all behind. It's not uncommon to hear the refrain in songs or in movies about leaving your neighborhood and never turning back. But there's also the yearning to make it something better, to not leave it behind.

We grow up underneath the palm trees, some of us left to our own devices, others warned against the dangers in the street. We learn to both love and fear these streets made of anger. Doused in sunshine, they look almost serene. Keepers of our secrets, witnesses to our small deaths. •

SOPLO CARDÍACO

BY TIMOTHY GOMEZ

Memoir Essay

#1. Syncopation

When I'm born, the doctor identifies a heart murmur.

The rapid flow of blood from one chamber to another. The sound it makes. An out-of-place hum.

My mother repeats this fact throughout my life, sometimes over Americanized hard shell tacos with ground beef, marinated lettuce, and cheddar cheese, sometimes over the television, the fifth time through the chocolate episode of *I Love Lucy*, sometimes while we dust the furniture of the sitting room she never allows anyone to sit in.

You were born with a heart murmur, mijo, she always tells me. *The doctor told me*, she says. But no other doctor I visit ever repeats this. I spend most of my life curious enough to wonder what a murmur means but not enough to find out.

Twenty-five years later, and not a single doctor mentions it again. I begin to wonder if Madre was lying or perhaps she misheard. I wonder if she used this as an excuse to treat me gently, with caution. For me to learn to treat myself the same. Gently. With caution.

To never move too quickly.

During a visit to a clinic that charges only twenty dollars for the physical my new school requires, the doctor holds his stethoscope, hard and cold, to my heart and says, *Hmm, sounds like you have a little heart murmur. Has anyone ever told you that?*

I nod, surprised.

It's nothing, though, he says. *If it hasn't caused you any problems yet, it probably never will.*

The rapid flow of blood from one chamber to another. The sound it makes.

An out-of-place hum.

Often harmless. The type I have is called an 'innocent murmur.' A 'function murmur.'

I joke one night to L while telling this story, *It basically means my heart is pumping too hard. My heart is just too much.* She rolls her eyes and smiles.

But the truth is, I find—to my comfort—that there's not much wrong with my heart at all.

#2. B IN THE CLASSROOM

B says he can't handle the quiet. He adjusts in his seat and smiles, stares down at his phone. *Why they all calm today, Mister?* he asks of the other students.

What's wrong with that? Isn't it nice for once?

Nah, he says.

He's been here for a month, with his heavy sweater in the California heat, with his wide-set frame, with his heavy stepping pattern, worn out Jordans, slow and steady, always late, pulling up his navy pants as he goes. He's been here for four weeks with his erratic laugh, sometimes soft and low, sometimes falsetto and exaggerated, his canyon smile. His eyes stuck in shadows.

Each day, I pull a stool next to his corner seat, the desk closest to the exit. Each day, we talk for twenty-five minutes. Each day, I ask him about his family, about how he likes being at a new school that's, as he puts it, always all in his shit, about his preference for being *out in the streets* with his friends. Between these questions that some days he answers with breadth, others with one word, I force a pencil in his hand and help him complete worksheets.

Fill in the blank.

Answer the question.

Don't forget your name, I tell him, pointing.

Why do you hate the quiet? I ask him.

I don't know. It's always noisy where I live. That's what I'm used to.

I tell him about my first apartment in New York. On Metropolitan Avenue in Queens. Below my room was a pizza shop and a well-trafficked produce store. At night, every night, garbage trucks would barrel through the streets firing off all sorts of sounds, metal machinery crunching against more metal, or compacting pounds upon pounds of the city's waste. On windy nights, the pizza shop's sign would sway outside my bedroom window, ungreased rusty metal sliding. Back and forth. For nights, I couldn't sleep, but my mind would eventually get used to the ruckus. Used to the late night sirens and horns. Used to the busses pulling over and lowering their doors while beeping.

When I would go home to my mom's, I tell B, *her house is on this quiet block, and my room was sealed off real well from everything, I wouldn't be able to sleep.* I tell him how I would toss around in bed. The covers each morning would be splayed like laundry. My eyes would water from the tired.

Yeah that's how it is, he tells me. *If it's that quiet, I think too much.*

What do you think about?

I don't know, Gomez, he tells me. *Dumb shit.*

He looks down.

After some quiet, B tells me he wants to leave this school. He says this at least twice a week.

When I ask him for a reason, he says, *Mister, I want to go to a school that has a little more—* and he pauses. He lets out a small but knowing, quiet laugh. *Craziness. A little more craziness.*

You don't like that this place has a little structure? I ask him.

I'm just not used to it, he says.

I suddenly feel deeply connected to B. And I could feel a thin layer between us melt away. My mentor J always tells me to work for this. To work to humanize the child in front of you. To work to humanize yourself in front of them.

I hate the silence too. I worry what the calm might mean.

B and I talk some more. I cannot convince him to want to stay at our school, so instead I offer to play him Connect Four. He hesitantly agrees. There is no resolution. In fact, there won't be. In just a few weeks, I don't know this, but B will no longer attend our school. I will never see him again.

In this moment, I tell B, *We'll talk again tomorrow?*

Sure, Gomez, he tells me.

#3. A CONVERSATION WITH L OUTSIDE A BOYLE HEIGHTS BAR

Are we just as bad as the gentrifiers? L asks as we walk up to a new bar in Boyle Heights.

We talk about the education. The exodus. The return. The ways in which we both did it. Both to New York and then, hesitantly, almost by force, back to East LA.

Ten years before, I packed up my old Honda Civic until its axle nearly buckled. Books and clothing and old notebooks and planners. I lodged a dog bed in between it all where Cocoa Bean could sleep. And D and I drove from Pasadena to Green River. Green River to Denver. Denver to Omaha. Omaha to Gary. Gary to Akron. Akron to Queens. And I woke up the next morning to start grad school at Sarah Lawrence, writing with almost no one that looked like me. No last names I recognized the accents of.

L did nearly the same just a few years after and made documentary films with women she adored.

We talk about the difficulty. We wanted degrees. We wanted to make a decent living. We wanted to pay off our student loan debt. We wanted to make our neighborhoods prettier. We wanted to feel comfortable in them, so we would no longer feel pushed away by them. We wanted there to be more restaurants, more bars, more bookstores. We wanted to be more successful than our parents before us.

But then we stop ourselves. And we come to this understanding: what if our concept of success is actually informed by generations of someone else's desires? Someone else's measurements?

What if this is why we feel so lost in our own lives?

What would success look like to our grandparents? Their grandparents? Our most distant ancestors in Durango and Zacatecas? Is it possible to rebuild something we know nothing of? Is it possible to reconnect to a part of ourselves we can't fully identify?

Can we exist, at once, in multiple moments? Here and somehow then? With our hearts and with theirs? With these spirits we wouldn't be able to recognize?

What do you think they would want for us? L asks me.

I can't begin to imagine, I say.

We enter the bar. We shoot a shot of tequila. And drink Tecates with lime until the bar begins to blur.

#4. At What Point in Time Does a Song Become an Oldie?

At what point in time does a song become an Oldie? Is it when two children, five and four, sit in separate cars driving in opposing directions, almost into each other, on Huntington Boulevard? The curve of the street lined in its middle with palm trees, on its North with a hill of beaten down apartment complexes.

One of these kids—a perfect part on the left side of his hair, curls matted down by cheap gel using a plastic comb—rides in the middle seat, although there is no one else in the back with him. A gray Subaru. He asks his mom on the passenger side if they can go to Target.

The other kid, tight dark brown bangs above sneaky, smiling eyes, sits in the seat where she can see her Tata driving, his mustache firm and not yet graying. K-Earth 101 on both of their radios, Smokey Robinson comes on and belts, *A love like ours is never ever free.*

The two cars pass right by each other.

Maybe it's when she's crying about leaving her middle school boyfriend for the summer. She's on the 10 freeway. Or maybe it's when he goes to the swap meet in Santa Fe Springs and walks through aisles of trinkets and secondhand gardening tools. Maybe it's when they almost meet with their grandparents, possibly in the Flower District or the alleys, their grandmothers shopping for cheap toys and clothes, birthday gifts for their cousins; their hands held tight and high, dragged through the loud crowds. Lullabies of Spanish pouring from everyone around them; each syllable sounds familiar but impossible to decode.

Is it when that little girl's Tata takes her to see *A Bowl of Beings* when she's perhaps too young; he plays "I'm So Proud" on the radio and tells her what Chicano Power means. Is it when that little boy sees his dad high on amphetamines for the first time, his mother drunk on tequila; they dance to The Originals until they tumble to the linoleum; the bouncing movements feel almost like a waltz.

Is it when that little boy and that little girl sit beside each other on a hill in Whittier, their eyes closed, breathing. They look over a city that, at once, feels like it belongs to them and feels like it belongs to everyone but them. They point out places they recognize. And places they can't quite see. The pan dulce shop she never went to. The library he only walked by. The market, now torn down, where they may have gone, simultaneously, with their mothers, on a Sunday evening. They list and list what they know now by heart, lyrics and street names and restaurants, and the little girl tells the little boy about her Tata. *He was a good man*, she says. I feel like I've been searching my whole life for another person who loves like he did. Sometimes I convince myself it was never real. The little boy says nothing but rubs the face etched in the marble lodged in the grass between where they sit, then he rubs the little girl's cheek with his thumb.

They close their eyes and hum off-key.

Life can never be exactly how we want it to be, but I can be satisfied just knowing that you love me.

#5. Ofrenda, or What Language the Spirits Might Speak

I wonder if maybe I've lost the language of the spirits. I wonder if I could ever find their tune. I wonder if I could ever return to them.

Or return them to me.

Maybe they've been speaking to me all along.

SOPLO CARDÍACO BY TIMOTHY GOMEZ

If I could only translate their offerings.

In the soil of Guanajuato.

In my off-key renditions of *Volver, Volver*.

In the perfect proportions of cilantro and onion in a dirty tub placed on a metal counter hanging off the side of the taco trucks in El Sereno.

In the way L looks up and smiles at me when she hears the song her Tata would hum to her when she was small. And in the way I dance the same sidestep every time.

In the way I and R and M and E and I all laugh over homemade carnitas cooked in too much lard.

In the way my mother sips her whiskey and wipes dust from unused tables.

In the way the kids in my classroom call me only by my last name.

Hey, Gomez. they all say, sometimes in unison.

In the soft hum of a heart that pumps a little too fast. •

LIVE FROM THE 2012 APOCALYPSE

BY JESUS CORTEZ

Memoir Essay

SUMMER 2012 WAS A TIME OF GREAT CHANGE AND PANIC—OR AT LEAST curiosity—for the possible "end of the world," as some people had interpreted the Mayan calendar that year. I was single, heartbroken, and immersed in the world of community organizing. That June, the president had announced the creation of the Deferred Action for Childhood Arrivals (DACA) program—surreal for those who would qualify and finally be able to work "legally." For others, such as myself, who did not qualify, it just meant waiting even longer. It was frustrating, but I dealt with it by staying involved. My mother had taught me to do things from the heart, and not just when they benefited me.

In late July, the back-to-back murders of two young, brown men, Manuel Diaz and Joel Acevedo, executed in the streets of Anaheim by police—had changed my life drastically. By then I had lost count of the people murdered by police. In March, it had been the shooting of Martin Hernandez that sparked resistance from the community. The murders in July only added anger to an already enraged community. *Justice for Manuel Diaz and Joey Acevedo* became the cause that united many in the streets of Anaheim from all walks of life: mothers, street warriors, activists, young men and women.

Days of protests turned into clashes with police on the night of July 24. People from all over the city gathered in the downtown Anaheim area, near Disneyland. The protest grew louder and louder. There was anger in the youth, and fear in the police line trying to box in protesters in the Guinida Lane neighborhood. It all seemed headed to a tragic conclusion. Young brown men, (some might say gang members), led the charge, risking physical harm, but making sure elderly women and children remained towards the back to protect them from possible police violence. Activists ran for safety as señoras and señores with brown skin, white hair, and tired faces attempted to protect children and babies in strollers.

The tension in that part of the city finally dissipated and the protesters moved closer to City Hall, on Anaheim Boulevard. There, crowds of people chanted, yelled, and insulted the large groups of riot police from different police departments in Orange County.

Afterwards, we returned with the crowd who continued to yell at the police and record their behavior in case they started shooting at us. Minutes later, more young men showed up in packed cars. They were angry. How could they not be? Most of the victims of police shootings in Anaheim looked like them: young, brown, and with short hair. There was a standoff between the young men and the police in front of a vacant building—the future site of the Packing House, a large indoor food court, which became a symbol of the continued gentrification of the downtown Anaheim area. On the next street over, the sound of gunshots could be heard. Rocks flew across the night sky, breaking the windows of the vacant building, to which the police responded by shooting indiscriminately. Rubber bullets and pepper balls flew as people ran for cover, while in the distance, the Disneyland fireworks lit up the sky.

That night, crowds ran all over downtown. More rocks flew towards the police; more yelling in frustration. Police occupied the downtown area—a true show of force, an occupying army.

Days passed and more small-scale protests took place, each with a ridiculous response from the city government. Local Latino leadership took to the Spanish news media to renounce all violent activity by the protestors, but not by the police—going as far as blaming "outside agitators," and claiming that people from Anaheim "did not act like that." Eventually one of those Latino "leaders" would become a city council member.

In time, a sense of normalcy was forced upon the community due to the overwhelming police response. The mothers and family members of the victims of police violence continued to seek justice through the courts. I went back to work with the undocumented community, but with a more expanded focus and with less fear of authority. In those days, I learned that not all activists are what they claim to be, and not all leaders lead by example. In the end, life continued in Anaheim, until the next time the city streets were claimed by the community.

As they did in February of 2017, after an off-duty cop fired a shot during an altercation with an Anaheim youth. And, again in June of 2020 when the people of Anaheim protested in solidarity with the Black Lives Matter movement after the murder of George Floyd in Minneapolis, among the many cases of Black murders at the hands of the police. In both cases, aside from symbolic gestures on behalf of the city, the police continued with their tactics of repression and increased presence—this time, going as far as implementing a curfew, proving again that the police in Anaheim, like across the U.S., serves to murder people of color and repress protesters when they demand justice; in 2012, they just seemed to have perfected their tactics. •

WHAT REMAINS IN A CITY RACISM BUILT

BY NIDIA BAUTISTA

Memoir Essay

SATURDAY NIGHT BEFORE THE MAYOR PLACED A STAY-AT-HOME ORDER FOR all of Los Angeles, mere hours before restaurants and bars were ordered shut, I visited Otomisan, a cozy home-style Japanese restaurant on First Street, considered to be the last of its kind in Boyle Heights. It was the middle of March, I had just gotten back to the city after traveling for three weeks, from Chicago to New York to Mexico City, and it was only after settling back in did I start to grasp the gravity of the pandemic.

Coronavirus cases were on an uptick and it looked like restaurants would be ordered shut any day, so we decided to support a local business on what I assumed might be my last dinner out in a while. Otomisan, just a few blocks from my parents' house in Boyle Heights, is a monument in its own right. The restaurant has been around since 1956, and my parents, who migrated here from Mexico in the 70s, have been patrons for years. It's harbored a loyal clientele base, local families and many who have since moved out of the neighborhood come here for the bento box lunches, crackling tempura and to bask in a piece of L.A. history. It's also got better parking than Little Tokyo, so it's an easy choice for great Japanese food if you live close by.

My boyfriend and I arrived at a mostly empty restaurant, only a pair of older Japanese women dined in the red vinyl booth next to us. Ominous news played on the television and hand sanitizer on the counter, soon to become omnipresent in every operating business during the pandemic, were signs that things were awry but I ordered a steamy bowl of udon noodles with veggie tempura, all of which I slurped up, unknowingly enjoying my last sit-down dinner for months.

In the time since then, we've been faced with a global health crisis that has upended life as we know it. Public health officials have recommended we employ physical distancing and protective equipment like face coverings to mitigate the spread of the virus, shutting down virtually all businesses and changing how we socialize. Gone are the days of bar-hopping with friends and weekly visits to beloved restaurants and cafés. But the human toll has been even more severe: to date 138,000 people have died nationally and 4,000 have died in Los Angeles County. It's also been a time of reckoning with racism and anti-Blackness. The murder of George Floyd by Minneapolis police on May 25 sparked global protests against police brutality which have splintered off into organizing for racial justice on multiple fronts. Thousands of protestors have taken over L.A. streets for weeks, in a powerful display of public solidarity against racism. During these months of quarantine and growing discussions about racism, I've thought much about how placemaking and racism intersects in Los Angeles, how racism has shaped this city.

Otomisan, now 44 years old, is a remnant of a not-so-distant past when the neighborhood was home to a large Japanese population that thrived in Boyle Heights leading up to World

War II when, on orders of the federal government, tens of thousands of Japanese residents were placed in internment camps. I grew up in Boyle Heights, a neighborhood besieged on all sides by freeways, with a history layered in multiple migration stories. It's been home to Jewish socialists that organized against police brutality in the 1920s and 1930s, and many buildings along Cesar Chavez Avenue housed Jewish social clubs and organizing meetings. Buildings have since been torn down or remodeled but an enduring monument is the Breed Street Shul, an orthodox Jewish synagogue once considered the largest of its kind west of Chicago. Japanese families, like our neighbors from across the street, also call this place home. The family patriarchs met in the Manzanar internment camp and when they were released after the war they settled into a house across the street from where my family would move into decades later. Our history here started when an uncle arrived in Boyle Heights in the 1960s as a Bracero, a temporary farm worker. Originally from Durango, in northern Mexico, my uncle would help my father migrate from Sonora in 1972. My dad remembers sleeping under a billowing Catalpa tree on rainy evenings in his brother's yard when he first arrived in Boyle Heights. While my older sister and I have moved away, and even lived abroad, this is the only neighborhood my 72 year old dad has ever really called home. He met my mom, a paisana from Durango, in this city in 1979, they would eventually move into the house next to my uncle's, and together my parents endured life here in the 80s and 90s. "Ni de aquí ni de allá," my mom jokes, neither from Durango or the United States, but certainly from Boyle Heights.

While it's true that this neighborhood is marked by migration and forged by the diversity of its residents over time, the history of the neighborhood, how it was shaped, who was allowed to live here, has more to do with racial capitalism than the rosier picture of the cultural melting pot, "the Ellis Island of the West," that it's often touted as being. L.A. is a city shaped by racism. The way neighborhoods were created and divided is a deliberately racist project.

L.A. neighborhoods like Boyle Heights were redlined by banks and local officials, deemed uninhabitable for wealthy white people, kicking off divestment from the community we still endure today. L.A. was mapped out racially, with white surveyors ranking communities like Boyle Heights and Watts in terms of "security" and "desirability," only to exclude thousands of residents from access to home loans, and restricting where poor people of color could live. Boyle Heights, for example, was suitable for poor, often immigrant, people only.

This racism has helped forge the community we see today, one that prides itself for preserving immigrant culture, that celebrates the mariachi musicians in their namesake plaza on Boyle Avenue and First Street, the same fame that draws writers to make this neighborhood the setting of popular web series tackling narratives about gentrification and family. There's a sense of community resiliency here, all while the residents continue to be pummeled by the forces of racist violence.

Today, the coronavirus pandemic is devastating Black and Brown communities. These are the communities with the highest mortality rates and face the highest unemployment during the onslaught of a new economic recession. Boyle Heights, for example, has among the worst COVID-19 rates in the county. What's worse, in addition to the threat of possibly becoming sick, residents deal with additional stressors, like the threat of eviction.

My parents own their house here in Boyle Heights—it took them decades to pay off the mortgage, but this small plot is theirs, and for now, they can stay here for the rest of their days. But the majority of L.A. families are tenants and face more uncertain futures. Everyday, L.A. neighborhoods inch deeper into gentrification and we witness the rampant displacement of low-income families, as Black and Brown people are evicted from their homes to make room for wealthier, usually white, tenants. Los Angeles politicians, like recently arrested former District 14 councilmember Jose Huizar, and developers have fueled gentrification for years. Gentrification is racist violence, one that's spread to erase Black,

POC and immigrant communities and culture.

From what I can tell, shops along Cesar Chavez Avenue and First Street, two of Boyle Heights' main streets, have kept chugging along during the pandemic. A family friend has kept her storefront open where she sells fabric, yarn, and art supplies, and has made face masks for $5 dollars a pop. She's a single mother and, having been excluded from federal relief funds because of her immigration status, her shop is what's kept her family going. Down the street, families buy from street vendors selling flower bouquets and fresh fruit on Cesar Chavez and Soto. While Los Angeles has placed a moratorium on evictions, landlords continue to hassle and threaten tenants for unpaid rent, some have even been evicted. L.A. residents are pulling together for small business owners. There are fundraisers for street vendors and mutual aid efforts to support people struggling with bills and rent. But infectious rates are trending upwards despite four months of quarantine so it's hard to tell how long people will need to endure the pandemic and the devastation that comes with it.

This is how inequality informs everyday lives, how we experience life in this city, the pandemic notwithstanding. Racism has informed how Los Angeles was built, it determines how we experience the pandemic and it is the subject of a long overdue reckoning that will have ripples through every industry and all of our relationships. There's just no escaping it.

People are toppling structures that should have never been erected. In the last few weeks, protestors have torn down monuments of colonizers and slaveowners, like the Junipero Serra statue in Placita Olvera, in growing rebellion toward the memorialization of violence. The San Gabriel Mission, built in 1771 on orders of Junipero Serra, and which memorializes the oppression of native culture and the murder of thousands of native people, had its roof burned off—perhaps a sign of the times.

There are other, less conspicuous, monuments like freeways, racist structures designed to segregate neighborhoods.The 5 freeway hovers over Hollenbeck Park, our neighborhood park built in 1892, the site of so many families' picnics, carne asadas, quinceñera photo shoots, and in the last few months, a space of reprieve from social isolation. I've recently gone on walks around the Hollenbeck Lake with my mom, eventually walking beneath the freeway, built in 1960, a brutal reminder that it was a political and deliberate choice to slice this neighborhood with freeways. These are once again remnants of the racist redlining practices and Boyle Heights is definitely not the only place shaped by this— it's ever present in our city's communities of color.

While I've reflected on racism's intervention in my neighborhood, my main concern these last few months has been to keep myself from contracting the coronavirus. I worry about keeping my parents healthy. I want my family to survive the pandemic, to overcome the crisis that so far has claimed the life of an aunt in Obregon, Sonora. I miss my life before the pandemic but there's no return any time soon, and that in fact a return isn't the way forward. We are witnessing the destruction of some of L.A.'s monuments, of the chipping away of histories that should be dismantled.

I look forward to seeing more racist structures crumble. Of walking into Otomisan again, of sitting inside a restaurant that ought to have disappeared after cycles of displacement, of helping support its survival. In the meantime I'll be ordering some udon to go, having the equivalent of Japanese caldo in the middle of summer, enjoying a socially distant, hot but comforting meal, enjoying these parts of home that endure. •

THE N-WORD IS STILL THE N-WORD OF THE WORLD

BY DEVYNITY WRAY

Memoir Essay

IT STARTED OUT INNOCENTLY ENOUGH. PRIOR TO VAL'S OUTBURST, IT WAS a regular day. I was in the fitting room folding all the clothes that had been tried on by customers at Joe Fresh's flagship store where I was then employed, on 43rd and 5th Avenue in Manhattan, a now defunct location. Other employees were constantly in and out, gathering the articles of clothing customers had lost interest in, otherwise known as "go-backs" in the retail world, and taking them out onto the floor to be once again sifted through and perused by our shoppers. This location was a multi-level building and Val had been tasked on this shift with running go-backs from the second floor where I was and taking them back downstairs.

We were busy and focused on our individual assignments working both independently and in tandem as the store was soon to close. The last of the customers were filing out. That's when, without warning, it happened:

"What's good my niggas?!" Val burst into the fitting room with a Cheshire cat smile at once greeting, stunning and disturbing us all. And I was all alone. There were several other employees in the fitting room from different ethnic backgrounds, but I was the only Black woman so— I was alone. I proudly don long locs, assert my heritage freely, and from daily banter among the staff, it was known that I'd majored in Africana Studies in college. If there was anyone in that moment that should have put Val in his place, it was me. I had established myself as the Black woman of that location. Kenny, a Guyanese-Indian, Ruth, an Asian, and Jozette, a Dominican from Washington Heights— all looked at me wondering what would happen next.

"What?!"

"What's wrong? What? I can't say that? Fuck that. I can say what I want. It's just a word. It's in all the rap lyrics. It's a free country...and it's been 400 years!!" Val kept saying that. He kept shouting 400 years. "Slavery has been over for 400 years!" This arbitrary number is something I'd heard thrown out before. This was five years ago. We actually just came upon the 400 year anniversary of when the first enslaved African stepped foot onto American land. Perhaps that's where the confusion lies. Chattel slavery ended in the United States in 1865. That was less than 200 years ago. The Voting Rights Act of 1964 was enacted after decades of lynching, protest, and segregation. My grandparents have gut-wrenching tales they could tell of how their humanity was daily challenged and denied. Black Americans are still recovering from slavery. I can spout this bevy of knowledge I have at my disposal now, but in that moment, I felt choked. I was flummoxed by Val's reckless pronouncement. It was as if Val had a machine gun fully-loaded with every reason white people feel the need to say the N-word and I was being hit with the barrage all at once. It was the first time I'd been in the presence of a white person who so openly used the word without apology or concern for the feelings of the others around him.

The dichotomy of the word is imprecise. It is both a Black pronoun and a pejorative term depending on who it is that you are talking to and to what degree. There are many variables to its use. On one hand, the N-word saturates Black rap music, comedy, and entertainment. It can serve as both a colloquial greeting and an accusatory epithet. As a part of the Black lexicon, the expletive can start a fight or be a battle cry for freedom. The National Association for the Advancement of Colored People, or the NAACP, held a symbolic funeral for the word. Oprah Winfrey has been extremely vocal about eliminating it from Black parlance, much to the chagrin of its proponents found mostly in younger Black generations—although a quote from elder comedian Paul Mooney resonates, "Everybody wanna be a nigga, but don't nobody wanna be a nigga." Rappers refuse to not use it, Eminem notwithstanding, defending our re-appropriation of the word to the death. I say it a lot. It made me wonder if Val had heard me say it and thought it was okay. Or was it just Kanye West's song "Gold Digger" that made him feel like saying this word that we Blackfolk had demanded he never say was now permitted. There were so many thoughts cascading through my mind as it was happening. I thought about Val and where he'd come from. In speaking to him previously I knew that he was a second-generation immigrant of Bulgarian descent.

I didn't know that there were social tiers to whiteness until seeing *Titanic*. Since Black people are, more often than not, on the lowest rung of any stratification anywhere in the world, these kinds of distinctions don't naturally occur to us. In *Titanic*, Leo and his Italian friend are treated poorly by the wealthier whites that took passage on the doomed vessel. I'd never seen white people treat other white people with such disdain and disgust. Bringing it back to my Blackness, I thought, well, Leo and his friend may have been among the first to be cast off in the bowels of the ship, but at least they were on the boat – and unchained no less. There were no Black people on the Titanic. America, for immigrants, is a symbol of freedom. The streets are paved with gold in American myth until they arrive and see what's true. The Statue of Liberty symbolizes a new and unencumbered opportunity to pursue happiness. For Black people in America, born citizens, the daily fight for our humanity and equality is something we still grapple with today. I can see now why Val thought it was okay to use this pejorative so freely. Freedom is different for his kind. Val, a second-generation Bulgarian American, was one of these types of whites. He was proud and adamant and ignorant of the struggle of Black people in America. He thought he knew what he was talking about. His people had fled here and prevailed. I really considered what it might be like to be an immigrant – to face adversity and yet still have your own language, culture, and community as a buttress for your survival in an unknown place. I thought about having ancestors that were paid for their work, underpaid perhaps, but paid nonetheless. I thought about having ancestors that spoke a different language from those they'd come to serve, but were allowed to read. There were huge institutional differences. The space between us was vast. It was on the laurels of this space that Val rested. I got hot inside and remained silent.

This incursion left me weak. It was far beyond the discomfort I'd witnessed among whites in my AP English class as we read Mark Twain with caution. They knew not to say it. They knew not merely because of some societal stronghold that grasped at their primal urge to say it. It was deeper than the talking to I had to give my white roommate Jason, a self-professed "wigger" for quoting DMX's song "Ruff Ryder's Anthem," which is one of the most nigga-laced songs one might ever hear. Val's audacity caused me to question everything. Was he right? Should it be okay for him to say? Had having it so inextricably woven into the fabric of our jargon come back to bite us in our collective asses at this moment in the fitting room at Joe Fresh?

Recently, Bette Midler tweeted that the "woman is the N-word of the world." The tweet was met with so much criticism and upset that she later apologized and deleted the tweet, which, she revealed, had been a quote from John Lennon and Yoko Ono's song of the same name. Women have it bad in the world, yes, but the niggers are still the niggers of the world. Black is still the new Black. Calling another group "the N-word" of anything is proof of the same. The use of the word is something Black folk have yet to fully unpack, and for good reason. We did not create the word. Our oppressors did that and they did it out of hate, contempt, and scorn. For that reason alone, Val should not have uttered it, even though I now understand why, from his position on the totem pole of whiteness, he thought he should be allowed. If I could go back in time, I would explain all of this to Val. Or maybe not. Maybe Val is just an asshole and nothing I would have said to him in that moment would have mattered anyway. We'll never know. •

ART + LIT INTERVIEWS

WHAT A BROWN GIRL MUST DO TO BE SEEN

INTERVIEW WITH POET BARBARA JANE REYES

Author of the forthcoming book *Letters to a Young Brown Girl*

BY NIKOLAI GARCIA

Barbra Jane Reyes was born in Manila, Philippines and raised in the San Francisco Bay Area. She came out of the spoken word scene in the mid-90s—one of those poets who had never even taken a creative writing class, just loved writing. She received a BA in Ethnic Studies from UC Berkeley, and then went on to earn an MFA at San Francisco State University. Since then she has published three chapbooks and six full poetry collections. Having worked with various publishers, from smaller publishers like Arkipelago Books to more well-known independent publishers like City Lights, Reyes is well known and respected among the West Coast literary community.

Her work first came to my attention in 2012 via Aztlan Libre Press, who is known mostly for publishing Chicanx writers. When I received her chapbook, I was surprised to see she was not Chicanx—but I was not disappointed one bit. Besides embracing popular culture in her writing, she is political in her approach and unapologetic in her style. Her new collection, Letters to A Young Brown Girl *(BOA Edition, Ltd.), stays true to her style, as a book aimed primarily at young Filipina women with poems that empower and uplift while tearing away at the patriarchy.*

Besides getting permission to republish three of the poems from her new book in this issue of Dryland, *I was also able to conduct a socially distant interview (via email) with the poet to talk about her new collection; its title, the publishing industry, and making mixtapes.*

Nikolai Garcia: Can you tell me about the title for your new collection, *Letters to a Young Brown Girl*? Did you have this title in mind before you began the process, or was it something that came much after you started work on the manuscript?

Barbara Jane Reyes: I believe I started with "Some Brown Girl," as a working title, with this refrain of "nobody cares about some brown girl," on loop in my head. It started as thoughts on standards of beauty, and the lengths to which women and girls go, in order to conform to mainstream ideals of beauty. What must a brown girl do, so that others will see her as beautiful?

I admit, all my Ulta and Sephora emails were starting to get to me; how much cash must we drop on beauty treatments? Writing in response to the text of beauty treatment advertisements, I realized I was writing more about what must a brown girl do, so that others will see her. I started to think more and more about all the times in my own young life I felt "un-pretty," and hence, invisible.

Regarding the current and final title, *Letters to a Young Brown Girl*: I had been collecting questions from other Filipinxs, mostly women, on social media, asking them what their questions were for me. So many of their questions had to do with writing as an "ethnic" person, and how to quell their own fears of their narratives being too "foreign," that no one would ever accept, read, and love them.

So there are a couple of threads here, about beauty and acceptance, validation by the dominant culture, this fear of rejection.

It wasn't until much later that one of my mentors, poet, and editor Nick Carbó pointed out my title as relating back to Rilke's *Letters to a Young Poet*. I'd only read excerpts of this when I was around 19, but this was relevant too, about why one seeks affirmation and validation from elsewhere.

Nikolai: I definitely saw your manuscript as a rebuke of European beauty standards, especially in that first section of the book. Something else I noticed in that first section, and throughout the book, was how you went after the María Clara image, which I understand to be the traditional, feminine ideal image in Filipino culture. I was hoping you could speak to this a bit as I feel that any person going up against old ideas and customs can relate to this?

Barbara: It's been a couple of decades since I read José Rizal's *Noli Me Tángere*, which is where María Clara comes from. Yes, she is considered, as you say, the traditional feminine ideal image in Filipino culture. She is light-skinned, golden-haired, virtuous, devout, self-effacing, and so forth. And when she is separated from the one she loves (she does this out of duty), she falls ill, and is eventually cloistered and ghastly.

María Clara is a tragedy. She is the product of colonial rape. Her father is a Spanish friar. There's no reason to be polite about it. I hate for this to be the ideal of what I or any other Pinxy should be.

For me, the only silver lining is that a work of literature can be this enduring and influential.

Nikolai: Speaking of literature, I want to go back to something you mentioned before, about how you put out a call for questions on social media and heard back from many young women with questions about writing. I was wondering if you thought this was a good sign—if this actually means that more POC women are pursuing careers as writers? Do you think POC writers have a better chance at getting published now, as opposed to when you first started, or do we still face the same challenges as before?

Barbara: I believe more WOC and Pinxys are pursuing careers in writing, and finding publication for a few reasons: the proliferation of small and independent publishers tapped into established distribution networks, writing retreats targeting BIPOC, and the proliferation of MFA programs. WOC and Pinxys are connecting with fellow writers, generating new writings and workshopping with conceivably more like-minded writers, and finding mentors with significant publication experience as authors and editors.

When I first started getting published, it was with DIY, local, Pilipinx, and Asian American publications. People still do this, and I love it. What has changed over the past couple of decades is the reach of the "small." Technology has enabled us to find one another despite geography and get to know one another's work. Digi-

"PEOPLE HAVE ASKED ME WHY I CAN'T JUST WRITE ABOUT OUR BEAUTY. THAT IS NOT MY STYLE."

tal printing and POD have lowered the cost of publishing, and so small and independent publishers can take on more prospective authors, and to print in smaller print runs. I've seen many authors bolstered by multiple print runs, all of which are in small batches, a couple hundred units per print run, certainly a change from the traditional 1000 copies-minimum print run, which some of the established independent publishers still do.

These numbers paint the more realistic response to the question of barriers facing WOC and Pinxy writers seeking publication, rather than paint a utopic picture of traditional and established independent publishers suddenly becoming "woke" to our communities' politics and aesthetics. There are pockets of progressively minded publishers and editors, and there is an entire traditional institution into which only a small, anointed few gain entrance.

As for "challenges" facing WOC and Pinxy writers, if you have seen the recent #PublishingPaidMe hashtag on Twitter, you can see the racial disparities in publishing. In independent publishing, especially for poetry, and outside of the mainstream publishing houses, cash advances in the tens of thousands, to hundreds of thousands are not common.

Nikolai: A delightful surprise to me in your new collection was the "Brown Girl Mixtape" section. I love when poetry borrows from pop-culture, and in that section it seems like each poem is inspired by a specific song. What inspired you to write this group of poems? Did you make many mixtapes in your teen years?

Barbara: Yes, I loved making mixtapes when I was younger! Part of the joy of it was its sheer surprise; we would cue up blank cassette tapes in our tape decks, listen to our favorite radio stations, and hope our favorite songs would play, and hope we could press the record button right on time, right after the DJ would stop speaking and right before the first lyrics of the song would begin. And then once we'd get to the end of Side-A, flip the tape to repeat on Side-B. And then we would use our best pens and our best handwriting to list song title and artist for each side, on the cassette insert. And then we'd create cover art with our fancy handwriting, illustrations, or magazine cut-outs. Very DIY zine-like, yes? Those mixtapes would become our summer soundtracks, or gifts to our BFFs, and to our romantic interests.

Or we'd borrow one another's albums, and record our favorite tracks. We'd do this after school, come over to one another's homes, do homework, and raid one another's record collections.

Dare I say this was my first experience with curation? Yes, yes I'll say that. I'll also say this was kind of a prelude to learning how to order poems in a full-length book manuscript. From first to last track, first to last poem, what is the movement you want to affect?

So, when I was writing the poems in the "Brown Girl Mixtape" section, I was thinking of that curation, and thinking of the songs and WOC artists whose works define(d) certain important times in my own Brown Girl life. I tried to go for some deeper cuts, because that's also very important to indie and DIY aesthetics.

Nikolai: I want to end this interview by asking about one of your recent blog posts where you're talking about your manuscript. You mention that this is the kind of poetry that you have always wanted to write: for brown girls, but pinay-specific, and you end it by writing, "I am jumping out of my skin for this work to reach them." I was hoping you could speak to what you mean by that? Thank you.

Barbara: Over the past couple of decades, my writing has gone in a lot of different directions. I can tell you when writing specifically for who I think of as my community, when I have written my speakers to directly address my fellow community members, I feel I am on the right track, doing what I mean to do. I feel like my work is most genuine here, no "bells and whistles"; I think of what I would have needed, an Ate steeped in community and letters to talk story with me, whether I was ready or not.

After my second book gained a readership I had never anticipated (in numbers and demographic), I found myself directing my work outward from my community, and into a readership and industry of people nothing like me. That is not a direction I am fond of writing or proud of, "explaining" myself to others not invested in ever empathizing — in short, writing for a white gaze, a contemporary American poetry publishing industry gaze.

Now, about "jumping out of my skin," I am just so eager for this book to be in the hands of Filipina/o/x readers. I don't know that everyone will "like" it; there are people in the community who have historically distanced themselves from my work because of my use of "foul" language, and because a lot of what I write is painful and violent. People have asked me why I can't just write about our beauty. That is not my style. •

FIND OUT MORE ABOUT THE POET ON TWITTER @BJANEPR
PRE-ORDER *LETTERS TO A YOUNG BROWN GIRL* ON BOOKSHOP.ORG

LIKE BULLETS FOR FASCISTS

INTERVIEW WITH POLITICAL POET MATT SEDILLO

Author of *Mowing Leaves of Grass*

BY VIVA PADILLA

Chicano revolutionary poet Matt Sedillo met up with me (proper masks were worn) in El Sereno in June to catch up and talk about his newest poetry collection Mowing Leaves of Grass *(FlowerSong Press, 2019). During this interview we drove around the Eastside. We came upon a squeaky clean Black Lives Matter/ Defund the Police protest in Pasadena, boarded up and tagged "R.I.P. George Floyd" storefronts in the belly of high gentrification in Highland Park, and the homeless encampment at the Veteran's Monument in El Sereno — a proper backdrop for the political insight Sedillo delivers like a gun-slinger in his book where American institutions rooted in white supremacy are dragged out by the hair and left on the side of the road to rot.*

Viva Padilla: Over the past decade you have built quite the reputation traveling the country and establishing yourself as a celebrated political poet. Much of your work is very historically dense and well researched. Why have you chosen poetry as the vehicle to get out your message?

Matt Sedillo: It wasn't so much a choice as something I really fell into. The reality is I learned all I know from a library card and Wi-Fi connection. My route into the movement came not through the academy nor a background in organizing but rather from writing poetry that tackled issues of class struggle, Chicano history, general US history, US imperialism, the destruction of the environment and various other issues and causes of our day.

There are some real advantages to being a poet in how fluid I have been able to move from rallies to conferences to performance to workshops to working with historians and journalists. For me poetry has always been more a vehicle than a destination but I do take the craft very seriously. I love fighting the good fight. I love writing poetry. I am a lucky guy to get to do both simultaneously.

"THE MELTING POT WAS NEVER MEANT FOR THE HANDS THAT CLEAN IT"

-PILGRIM

Viva: Your latest collection is entitled *Mowing Leaves of Grass*. Why did you choose to go after Walt Whitman and have you have gotten any blowback?

"I AM FEUDALISM
I AM SLAVERY
I AM THE FREE MARKET
I AM THE ONE PERCENT
I AM CAPITALISM
AND I WILL WATCH YOUR CHILDREN STARVE
TO SATISFY MY GREED"

-THE DEVIL

Matt: "What has miserable, inefficient Mexico—with her superstition, her burlesque upon freedom, her actual tyranny by the few over the many—what has she to do with the great mission of peopling the new world with a noble race?" - Walt Whitman

That is a direct quote and there is no context to rectify it. The book is largely about the Rebrowning of America and the political response, namely the rise of Trump and his base of support.

As to backlash, white liberals in the literary community have attacked it on a few occasions as many of them see Walt Whitman and Donald Trump as polar opposites. I am Mexican, Chicano, I make no distinctions between anti-Mexicans.

I think Walt Whitman was talented. But he was a racist who hated Mexicans among others. I am also talented. Lots of us are. You're very talented. The authors you publish are very talented. Our community does not need to look up to the Walt Whitmans of the world. We do not need to look up to people who look down upon us. Our efforts would be better spent seeking out, supporting and fostering the genius from within our own community.

Viva: Who are you trying to reach with this book?

Matt: In many ways *Mowing Leaves of Grass* represents my Chicano studies book. It has found a home with radical educators much more so than the literati and I am happy with that. I want people who share these politics to get the book and feel engaged and ready to contribute to the struggle. As a political poet I really want to rally people and ignite their passions. If they are encouraged to further research some of the allusions made in the poems all the better; my primary goal, however, is always to rally people to fight.

"THE BOYS IN BLUE
THE KILLING CREW
AUTHORIZED LYNCH MOB
DEATH SQUAD
AMERICA SIGNED WITH A BULLET
FIVE PIGS TO ONE TEENAGER
HANDS CUFFED BEHIND HIS BACK
LOUD PROUD FRAT BOYS WALK BY
DRINKING FROM FLASKS
BLACK YOUTH IS CRIMINALIZED
WHITE CRIME
IS STATE SANCTIONED"

-ONCE

Viva: You are published under FlowerSong Press who have been doing dope work in Texas. How did this working relationship come about and what has your experience been?

Matt: With a handshake. Edward Vidaurre and I were booked for an appearance at UCLA. He was staying with his mom in Boyle

Heights. I picked him up and we just started talking—next thing I knew I had a deal with FlowerSong.

As to being on the press, the experience has been incredible. It's a growing press with a lot of ambition. In the coming years FlowerSong is a place where legends will be made. I have no doubt about that.

Viva: Anything else in the works?

Matt: Yes. I am working on a few all to be published with FlowerSong. My next title is going to be called *City on the Second Floor*. If *Mowing Leaves of Grass* is my Ethnic Studies book then *City on the Second Floor* is very much my poetic foray into Marxist Geography. Look out for it next year. •

ORDER MOWING LEAVES OF GRASS ON FLOWERSONGPRESS.COM

MAKING THE PAST
PRESENT

INTERVIEW WITH ARTIST PATRICK MARTINEZ

BY MICHAEL LORENZO PORTER

Photo by Viva Padilla

July 1st, Stockton, New Jersey. A week away from my current home (Brooklyn) has placed me in the countryside of New Jersey. It's peaceful here, but even as birds chirp and power saws lop off chunks of wood in the distance of another cloudless summer day, I know that this is only an illusion of peace. This country, and to a larger extent, the world, is on fire...

I scroll Twitter briefly as I prepare for my interview with Patrick Martinez. His work, which consists of neon, sculpture, and landscapes is deeply inspired by the varied Los Angeles terrain and wide-ranging cultures that make the city a truly diverse place. As a fellow native Angelino, protests, mass unrest, and a fascist in office, we had plenty to talk about. I place myself in a quiet, air-conditioned room and dial Patrick's number...

Porter: Thanks for taking the time to talk to me, Patrick. I want to start at the beginning. You were born in L.A. at the beginning of the 80s... Can you talk to me about growing up in that time and how art came into your life.

Patrick Martinez: I grew up in San Gabriel Pasadena California. So in the 80s and 90s it was a very different place than it is now. My earliest art memory was of me making things in kindergarten for my mom on Mother's Day. I was making things with tissue paper and bottles and I really liked to use clay—I liked how it felt. I remember not being able to articulate how I felt while working but there was a sense of gratification, while I was sculpting or cutting; there was a stillness that I felt at no other time. So I felt very calm when I was making these things. I felt accomplished. I remember when the other kids would be done and they would just kind of get through it. I was taking my time and wanting the piece to match the idea I had in my head. That continued and carried over into drawing from ob-

"MALCOLM X SAID THEY WILL TELL YOU THAT YOU ARE HATEFUL FOR BRINGING UP THESE TRUTHS. THE TRUTH IS THAT THEY NEED TO TAKE A LONG LOOK IN THE MIRROR AND WE NEED TO [DO THAT] AS A COUNTRY, WE NEED THERAPY, WE NEED TO FACE THE PAST SO WE CAN MOVE FORWARD."

servation; things on TV, cartoons, comic books and I was really just training my eye to see what was there and then trying to translate that into 2D drawings. Those were very early stages and then when I turned 11 or 12, I started trying to manipulate spray paint onto a wall because I saw it on the subway art and in books that I would see in middle school. Simultaneously, my brother, who was just two years older, he was tagging a lot and he and his friends sort of adopted me into that culture. Then I found peers my own age in school, we had a crew, and we'd take the bus all over town and do graffiti in new places. So those experiences had a big impact on how I view landscapes, the different people living in the different pockets of L.A.

Porter: It's interesting that you talk about the pockets and different people and cultures. Everyone knows how diverse L.A. is but as someone who is from L.A., you understand that the geography of the city does lend itself to being isolated and a feeling of being separate. You kind of have to travel to get outside your bubble.

Patrick Martinez: What activated my current art was the energy of graffiti. My brother's friends would be over, they'd have markers and shit and I said "Hey, that's art?" Their materials were a lot like mine. So my parents would be out of town in Vegas and we'd have friends over and we would draw in the black books. That really got me exploring color and scale and what the message of what I'm doing actually was. I think as young as 12, I was doing graffiti around town pretty consistently. I can look back on these experiences now and say yes, they were very formative as far as my art goes.

Porter: That time period that you're talking about: the early 90s were very turbulent in Los Angeles. I suppose this is also a turbulent one as well. Can you talk to me about growing up through that?

Patrick Martinez, Los Angeles, CA. July 2020

Photo by Viva Padilla

"WE DIDN'T DO THE RESEARCH AT 11, 12 YEARS OLD BUT LATER ON WE CAME TO THE REALIZATION THAT THAT EVENT WE LIVED THROUGH WAS NOT A NEW THING OR A FIRST TIME THING. WE GREW UP TO LEARN OUR REALITIES WERE KIND OF A REPEAT."

Patrick Martinez: I saw the Rodney King beating on TV when I was 11 years old. I understood it. I knew what was going on. And by 12 years old, there was the uprising. So literally outside of my brother's and my window you could see smoke about 5 blocks away. And it was very surreal to see smoke emanating from a building just down the street while seeing all these things unfold live on TV at the same time. They burned a strip mall area too. The music mirrored the time as well. We felt it all coming together. We didn't do the research at 11, 12 years old but later on we came to the realization that that event we lived through was not a new thing or a first time thing. We grew up to learn our realities were kind of a repeat.

I didn't necessarily get into art to be some kind of rebel or some type of counterculture person, you know? It was just a reaction to the things that were happening around me. It meant wearing a shirt or writing a message on a wall.

Porter: I am a few years younger than you so my memory of these events is a little more abstract. Hearing you talk about the 90s and specifically the 1992 uprising, I can vividly remember my mom coming home with a basket full of potatoes and thinking why did mom only buy potatoes and why is Vons on fire? So it's great to hear the perspective of someone who had a better grasp of the moment.

Patrick Martinez: Yeah, and this is the work that I do. When I do these interviews it's actually, it helps me to realize that these are things that inform the work now, music and key moments and moments of American history that inform the content of my work and it's kind of an organic thing. Those things could have not happened, and then I wouldn't have an opinion. It's interesting to talk about this because I can talk about it while someone is checking out a piece of work at a gallery. It's nice to reiterate to readers or people that are listening.

Porter: What you say makes me think of something. As you're getting close to finishing a piece of work, whether it be collage, clay, or neon, is it important to you that people understand your finished work? Is it important to you that they feel anything at all? How does reaction play into your process?

Patrick Martinez: I think it's not anything specific that they should get from a piece. Negative feelings are just as valid as positive feedback or feelings. I appreciate when that person from Orange County who is living inside of a bubble comes at me and says "This piece is race-baiting" or "This is hateful" because at least they are thinking about the topic I am addressing on some level.

Porter: I also want to ask you. You said that it is occurring to you now that you're living through American history. That's also true of today. How does that make you feel, to know that you are making something that is speaking to or documenting a moment in a sense? Do you feel pressure to encapsulate everything or is it more about how you feel at a certain time specifically?

Patrick Martinez: I guess what I'm trying to say about the past, or the recent past I should say, because I don't feel like it was a long time ago in terms of the measure of history: I like to try and make the past PRESENT. There are things that I am reiterating that I have witnessed, people being harassed and murdered by police etc. The work that I make I want to accurately represent the time that I live in, that we all live in. I don't know if I do a great job all the time and I'm still working on certain ideas but my whole goal is to represent the time period well. The Pee Chee folders are a kind of bridge from where I'm at to the general population or if I want that idea or those kind of memorial pieces to be seen by, to connect with as many people as possible because these killings are happening and we should not forget these things.

Porter: I saw the design for the Pee Chee folders and I was immediately connected to a very nostalgic time, as a 5-year-old living in L.A. with my mom and my little brother. But also I think it does a very good job of connecting those times with now because you have the image of George Floyd and Breanna Taylor on the front and they were just killed this year and so I

"THINK ABOUT IT. IF A YOUNG CHILD NEVER SEES THE WORK OF SOMEONE LIKE THEM, THEY AREN'T GOING TO GRAVITATE TOWARDS WANTING TO PARTICIPATE IN THAT ART FORM. THEY MAY THINK THERE IS NO PLACE FOR THEM, THEY MIGHT NOT UNDERSTAND IT. "

Patrick Martinez, Los Angeles, CA. July 2020

Photo by Viva Padilla

think by putting them into this form of the school folder and taking people back, you're kind of asking the question: "What's the difference between 2020 and 1992?" and if that's the case, what's the difference between 1776 and 2020? And obviously things have changed since then but we should be a lot farther along than we are.

Patrick Martinez: Absolutely. I feel like reflections of people that don't want to see this. They can't really say anything about it because it's not like I'm making this up. These are real people and they lived so the people who don't want to face their past don't want to face their reality. Malcolm X said they will tell you that you are hateful for bringing up these truths. The truth is that they need to take a long look in the mirror and we need to [do that] as a country, we need therapy, we need to face the past so we can move forward.

Porter: What do you think is our biggest roadblock right now to progress in terms of art institutions representing the full spectrum of artists living in the United States? As it stands right now, most of the people on the boards don't look like me and you, and I don't mean progress as like meeting a diversity officer because that never works.

Patrick Martinez: Right, it becomes a box that you can just check. I don't know all the answers but I think that there are connections in these institutions so if we say a white suprema-cist, capitalist, patriarchal element exists in America, of course it's in the museums and the institutions that are telling us what artists to buy and pay attention to. If we can affect the bigger picture, hopefully you will start to see inclusion in the museums. There is only so much that the curators can do. I know a lot of them and a lot of the people on the boards have an agenda of what they want to show and push. I mean, look at The Whit-ney.

It doesn't have a lot to do with what me or you would want to see in a museum. Think about it. If a young child never sees the work of someone like them, they aren't going to gravitate towards wanting to participate in that art form. They may think there is no place for them, they might not understand it. I'm not talking about supremacy. I'm talking about equality. A sense of things being fair and that's what I mean in terms of institutions being equal and representing everyone. It's not there [yet] but it feels like there is progress now and curators are putting in work but sometimes you hit a wall. They are going to need help from us.

Porter: I agree. I think it is going to take some time but I am hopeful that we could see more representation in our lifetimes.

I also wanted to ask you. Do you remember what it was like to sell your first piece?

Patrick Martinez: Probably a deal to a friend or something. Officially through a gallery? I can't remember but I do remember feeling like I had caught a rhythm of things being sold and feeling like wow, I can pay my bills and that was like not long ago, let's say 2015.

Porter: Prior to finding that rhythm, what was the thing that kept you making art?

Patrick Martinez: It's an autotelic thing. It's just automatic that I have to make stuff so it has nothing to do with this economy or a need to make money. I have worked jobs in the past for the sole purpose of supporting my art. I've worked at agencies and things like that. That's not an issue, it's more of wanting to be able to spend all my time on doing this. I enjoy putting stuff out there that didn't exist before and getting a response. That's the meaningful thing for me. I like the idea of making something that takes up space and then having a group respond to it. Obviously money is great in the context of capitalism but it was never the reason I was making anything.

It's important not to measure yourself against another person. Your work is something that needs to be watered and there is no booklet on making a piece of art like there is a booklet on how to drill a cavity or pull a tooth out. This is not a regular thing to do.

Porter: I wanna talk about some of your wall collages because when I first heard about you, I didn't know that you made wall collages.

Patrick Martinez: Those are landscapes and when I paint landscapes, I had been trained traditionally to think about atmospheric perspective, color, value but with these they are all inspired by different pockets of L.A. but I'm using still atmospheric perspective but with objects and texture and color and I'm taking 4-5 different places and putting them all into one. I'm using banners, stucco, security bars to push and pull the landscape. So these are things I'm thinking about when I'm making these wall pieces. These are explorations of the land.

"IT'S IMPORTANT NOT TO MEASURE YOURSELF AGAINST ANOTHER PERSON. YOUR WORK IS SOMETHING THAT NEEDS TO BE WATERED AND THERE IS NO BOOKLET ON MAKING A PIECE OF ART LIKE THERE IS A BOOKLET ON HOW TO DRILL A CAVITY OR PULL A TOOTH OUT. THIS IS NOT A REGULAR THING TO DO."

Porter: Who are some of your influences in art?

Patrick Martinez: So my influences are my surroundings, the people and places, firstly. And that's why my work is urgent. Having said that, artists inspire me. My peers inspire me. When I was a teenager I would look at Basquiat, Keith Haring, they were doing graffiti like I was doing so they were huge to me. Later on, it became people who were producing work alongside me. I like artists who simultaneously add something new to the conversation while continuing the story. Like, when you look back, you can't tell the story of this time without them.

Porter: What's your favorite movie?

Patrick Martinez: For me, during these times when I want to es-cape, I'll just watch some trash on TV. I am trying not to watch a lot of violent content right now but if I want a beautiful visual that moves, I love Michael Mann movies. I feel he captures the landscape of L.A. honestly. Most L.A. filmmakers will talk about cliché things like congestion or something like that but Mann gives you the opposite of that, he deals with emptiness and isolation very well I think. His films are very sultry, handsome por-traits of the city. I'm somewhat biased because I like to be out-side in open land and I love night scenes with lights twinkling and shit like that.

PORTER: How are you dealing with this collective idea that time doesn't matter, do you feel you have more time or that you have less?

Patrick Martinez: I think it's great that we have this moment to reflect together. I think we have all slowed down, like a hard reset, and then the uprising happened. So we went from being in total solitude to being super social and outdoors with people. Right now, I feel like I am still trying to get used to a slower pace. I don't keep a riguous studio schedule. Sometimes I'm thinking about ideas, sometimes I allow a couple days off. I am just try-ing to be mindful and listen. I used to go to the studio six times a week and didn't really give myself time to breathe. So I'm trying to practice self-preservation just so that I am healthy and able to function. This time has taught me that. So I am trying to be okay with doing nothing for a period and then going back into a piece with a new mindset. This idea of slowing down is something that I've considered before but have really put into practice with the shutdown and the time since we have all had to deal with and accept as everyday life. •

FIND OUT MORE ABOUT THE ARTIST ON IG @PATRICK_MARTINEZ_STUDIO

CONTRIBUTORS

Nidia Bautista is a writer and journalist from Boyle Heights. Reporting on immigration and gender justice. Found belonging in the transbarrios and that's often where she writes and thinks from. Collective storytelling on @PochaPunks and *Pocha Punks Power Hour*, a community radio show.

Xochitl-Julisa Bermejo is the daughter of Mexican immigrants and the author of *Posada: Offerings of Witness and Refuge* (Sundress Publications, 2016). She has work published in *The Acentos Review, CALYX,* and *crazyhorse* among others. She is a cofounder of Women Who Submit.

Carolina C. Blanchard is a Panama-born, Latinx, agender author, living in Los Angeles, CA. Current projects include their first poetry collection. They also have a degree in Fashion Design and have participated in writing classes and workshops.

Anthony J. Cassarino recently obtained his BA from California University of Pennsylvania. He majored in English with a concentration in creative writing. He could write before he could read. His hobbies include gaming, adventuring, and of course, writing.

Jessica Ceballos y Campbell is the daughter of magicians, granddaughter of a nest of dragonflies, and great granddaughter of a brown bear. She also just launched @alternativefield, a poetry library and resource center. jessicaceballos.com

Juliana Chang is a Taiwanese American writer and filmmaker. She is the recipient of the 2019 Urmy/Hardy Poetry Prize, the 2017 Wiley Birkhofer Poetry Prize, and a 2015 Scholastic Art & Writing Gold Medalist in Poetry.

Alan Chazaro is the author of *This Is Not a Frank Ocean Cover Album* (Black Lawrence Press, 2019) and the forthcoming *Piñata Theory* (Black Lawrence Press, 2020). He is currently a creative writing adjunct professor at the University of San Francisco and is a writer and editor of NBA stories at *HeadFake* on Medium.

Jesus Cortez is an undocumented immigrant writer and poet. His poetry has appeared in *The Acentos Review* and the *2017 Chicon Street Poets Anthology*. He was honored as a 2017 runner-up for the Chicon Street Poets "Give Me Something Else" Chapbook Prize. He lives and works in West Anaheim, California.

Iliana Cuellar is an L.A. native born to Salvadoran immigrants. Her work explores diaspora, feminine wiles, and love between borders and binaries. She is currently working on her PhD in Comparative Literature at UC Riverside, where she focuses on Latin American and French literary and visual cultures.

Jade Daniels is a movement artist, healer, organizer, storyteller, and so much more. Daniels utilizes words, movement, space, and time to create, connect, liberate, and experience. They believe truthful storytelling and healing are critical pathways to liberation. And that every nigga is a STAR.

Holly Day's poetry has recently appeared in *Asimov's Science Fiction*, *Grain*, and *Harvard Review*.

Giana De Dier (b. 1980, Panama). Her work turns to mixed media collage and digital compositions that combine both archival and contemporary photos paired with a variety of objects and environments of shaping a persona and navigating personal space. She studied Visual Arts at the University of Panama and has shown her work locally and internationally.

Roberto Alfonso Díaz is a partner, father, and activist living in Boyle Heights with his partner Thali and their two children Yol and Nina. He was a 2018 Community Literature Initiative Fellow and is completing his debut collection of short stories *Fictions Y Fabulas*. IG: @xicanowriter

Linda Dove holds a PhD in Renaissance literature and teaches college writing in Southern California. Her award-winning poetry books include *In Defense of Objects* (2009), *O Dear Deer,* (2011), *This Too* (2017), and *Fearn* (2019). She is the faculty editor of *MORIA*, the national literary magazine of Woodbury University.

Olga García Echeverría. Proud daughter of immigrants. Born and raised in East Los Angeles. Author of *Falling Angels: Cuentos y Poemas*. Maestra of literature. Creator and destroyer of language. BA in Ethnic Studies. MFA in Creative Writing. Honorary degree in code-switching from La Universidad Autónoma de Lenguas Desbordadas.

Biko Eisen-Martin is a bicoastal actor, painter, and award-winning slam poet. bikoeisenmartin.com

Tongo Eisen-Martin is a poet, movement worker, and educator originally from San Francisco. His latest curriculum on extrajudicial killing of Black people, "We Charge Genocide Again," has been used as an educational and organizing tool nationwide. His book, *Someone's Dead Already*, was nominated for a California Book Award. His latest book, *Heaven Is All Goodbyes*, (City Lights Pocket Poets series) was shortlisted for the Griffin Poetry Prize and won both a California and American Book Award.

Aaron El Sabrout is a transgender alien currently living on Tewa territory. He is a poet, gardener, artist, activist, and lawyer. His self-published poetry, comics, and short fiction can be found @ toreachpoise on IG, along with pictures of his radishes.

Jo Foderingham-Brown (she/her/he/him) is a Black, queer, gender non-conforming woman from Georgia, currently living in D.C. She has been writing since childhood and started performing her work in 2016. Common subjects of her work are misogynoir, Blackness, interpersonal relationships, and her Jamaican heritage. IG & Twitter: @tallawahgram

e.m. franceschini was born in Puerto Rico and is a former day laborer and U.S. Army veteran who now holds a PhD from UC, Berkeley and is an Assistant Professor of English and Latin American Studies at the University of Georgia. His poetry has appeared or is forthcoming in *Somos en escrito, Moko, Chiricú*, among others.

Nikolai Garcia grew up in South Central L.A., but has been living in Compton for almost two decades. His poems have been published in *Latino Book Review, Huizache, Cultural Weekly, Drunk Monkeys, Sad Girl Review*, and other literary journals. His first chapbook, "Nuclear Shadows of Palm Trees," was released by DSTL Arts.

Timothy Gomez is an English and Ethnic Studies teacher in Los Angeles, California. He holds an MFA from Sarah Lawrence College. His essays have appeared in *No Tokens, The Boiler Journal, Mixtape Memoirs*, and others. IG & Twitter: @timfinitely

Jordan Green is from Monroe, Louisiana, and is currently earning an MA in Creative Writing from the University of Louisiana Monroe (ULM). Presently, Green is working on a collection of poetry and flash fiction. They plan to attend Miami University in Oxford, Ohio for their MFA in Poetry.

Lituo Huang lives in Glassell Park. She is the author of "This Long Clot of Love," a chapbook of poetry and short fiction. Her work has appeared in *JMWW, Bosie Magazine*, the *Recenter Press Poetry Journal*, and elsewhere. She is writing her first novel. Twitter: @LituoH

William J. Joel. All things are connected. That's the premise of what William J. Joel does. Each of his interests informs each other. Mr. Joel has been teaching computer science since 1983 and has been a writer even longer. His works have recently appeared in *Common Ground Review, DASH Literary Journal*, and *The Blend International*, among others.

Abraham A. Joven is a writer and immigrant rights advocate in Southern California. His writing has been featured in *The Rumpus, Catapult,* and *k'in,* among others. He loves his wife, daughter, and Liverpool Football Club.

Wasabi Kanastoga is a Cuban-born poet raised in Los Angeles. His poetry has appeared in various anthologies and reviews. He is a counselor working with victims of abuse at a non-profit in Los Angeles.

Claire Kooyman lives in Boulder, Colorado with her cats, Tom and Finn. She graduated from University of Colorado Boulder in 2018 with a degree in creative writing. She has been published in *Not Your Mother's Breast Milk* and she recently completed an editorial internship with *Cleaver* magazine.

Teka Lark is a poet, essayist, and fiction writer from Los Angeles who currently lives in New York.

Tricia Lopez is a Nicaraguan and Salvadoran writer from Los Angeles. She is the former Editor-in-Chief of *MORIA Literary Magazine* and has had her work published in *Cultural Weekly, Athena,* and *Rabid Oak*. She is getting her MFA in Creative Writing at Mount St. Mary's University. She also has a podcast titled *It Girl Thoughts*. IG: @trvcvv.l

Christian Hanz Lozada is the product of an immigrant Filipino and a Daughter of the American Revolution. He co-authored the poetry book *Leave with More Than You Came With* and the history book *Hawaiians in Los Angeles*, and soloed shorter works published in places like *A&U Magazine* and *Spot Lit*.

Alexandra Martinez is a baker and poet living in the tumbleweeds of Southern California. IG: @alxndramartinez & Twitter: @mexicanpiggybnk.

Patrick Martinez was born and raised in the San Gabriel Valley. His upbringing and diverse cultural background (Filipino, Mexican, and Native American) provided him with a unique artistic lens. Martinez cultivated his art practice through graffiti, which later led him to the Art Center College of Design, where he earned a BFA with honors in 2005. His work resides in collections at the Los Angeles County Museum of Art, the Smithsonian National Museum of African American Art and Culture, and the Cornell Fine Arts Museum, among many others; he has been covered by the *L.A. Times*, KCRW, and *Wired*, among others. In 2020, Patrick was awarded a residency at the Robert Rauschenberg Foundation. Patrick lives and works in Los Angeles, CA.

Jenise Miller is a Black Panamanian urban planner and writer from Compton. She is a Pushcart-nominated poet and Voices of Our Nations Arts (VONA) alumna. She is the author of the poetry chapbook "The Blvd' and has published work in *KCET Artbound, Boom California, Cultural Weekly, Dryland Literary Journal,* and *The Acentos Review*.

Briana Muñoz is the author of *Loose Lips*, a full-length poetry collection published by Prickly Pear Publishing. Her work has also been published in the *Bravura Literary Journal, La Bloga*, the world's longest established Chicanx literary blog, and the *Oakland Arts Review*, among others. When she isn't typing away, she enjoys traveling, live music, cats, and thrift stores. IG: @awomanofwords

Viva Padilla is a poet and writer from South Central L.A. She has had her work feature in places like the *L.A. Times, PANK, The Autry, The Acentos Review, L.A. Forum for Architecture and Urban Design* among others; and has read at Casa de las Americas in Havana, Cuba. She is currently working on a poetry collection.

Iurhi Peña runs Beibi Creyzi, a queer feminist publisher of risography and screen printing that publishes graphics of women and sex-diverse people from Mexico and Latin America. She participates in the traveling library of feminist fanzines made in different parts of Mexico, Latin America and Spain that is run by the collective Autoeditoras: Hacemos Femzines, of which she is a part. She also teaches drawing and desktop publishing workshops.

Mr. Pintamuro is an artist of the Little Village neighborhood in Chicago, IL, currently working as a freelance muralist and illustrator. He has collaborated with nationally recognized Chicago interdisciplinary artists. He also works on site-responsive projects in Mexico, where he hosts workshops to create installations by pushing cross-cultural examination, history, cultural mobility, and indigenous sovereignty and sustainability. You can find mr.pintamuro's murals in Chicago throughout the 26th street corridor as well as a recent installation on 630 W Roosevelt Rd.

ANTHNYXYZ is a multidisciplinary artist from Compton, CA who specializes in portrait painting and mural art. His work centers Black men and places them in holy, saint-like images. Anthonyxyz has exhibited work in gallery spaces all over Los Angeles & NYC and, in the last four years, has completed nearly 10 murals throughout L.A. County.

Michael Lorenzo Porter is a writer, and visual artist originally from Mid-City L.A. Looking to subvert the widely expected myth in all its forms. His essays, interviews, and fiction work can be found published in print and online with *LARB, Hyperallergic, Cultured Magazine,* among others.

Monique Quintana is a Xicana writer from Fresno, CA and the author of the novella, "Cenote City" (Clash Books, 2019). She has received fellowships from Yaddo, The Mineral School, Open Mouth Poetry, and the Sundress Academy of the Arts. Her work has been nominated for Best of the Net and the Pushcart Prize. Twitter: @quintanagothic

Eva Recinos is a freelance writer and editor based in Los Angeles. As an arts and culture journalist, her work has been featured in *Hyperallergic, Los Angeles Times, Jezebel*, and more. Her non-fiction writing has appeared in *Electric Literature, Catapult, Marie Claire*, and more.

henry 7. reneau, jr. is the author of the poetry collection, *freedomland blues* (Transcendent Zero Press) and the e-chapbook, "physiography of the fittest" (Kind of a Hurricane Press). He has self-published a chapbook entitled "13hirteen Levels of Resistance," and his collection, *The Book Of Blue(s): Tryin' To Make A Dollar Outta' Fifteen Cents*, was a finalist for the 2018 Digging Press Chapbook Series. His work has also been nominated multiple times for the Pushcart Prize and Best of the Net.

Luivette Resto was born in Aguas Buenas, Puerto Rico but proudly raised in the Bronx. Her two books, *Unfinished Portrait* and *Ascension*, are published by Tía Chucha Press. She is a CantoMundo fellow. Her third book of poetry, *Promises Are Coffee*, is forthcoming from FlowerSong Press.

Tatiana Retivov received a BA in English Literature from the University of Montana and an MA in Slavic Languages and Literature from the University of Michigan. She has lived in Kyiv, Ukraine since 1994, where she runs an art & literature salon and a small publishing press, Kayala Publishing, that publishes prose, poetry, and non-fiction in Ukraine. Go to: kayalapublishing.com

Barbara Jane Reyes was born in Manila, Philippines, and raised in the San Francisco Bay Area. She is the author of six books of poetry, most recently *Invocation to Daughters* (City Lights Publishers, 2017) and *Letters to a Young Brown Girl* (BOA Editions, Ltd., 2020).

Kevin Ridgeway is the author of *Too Young to Know* (Stubborn Mule Press). Recent work has appeared in *Slipstream, Chiron*

Review, and *The American Journal of Poetry,* among many others. He lives and writes in Long Beach, CA.

Nick Rossi is a co-founder/editor/designer at *Sobotka Literary Magazine,* Ursus Americanus Press, and No Rest Press. His work has recently appeared in *Columbia Poetry Review, Funny Looking Dog Quarterly,* and *Travelin' Appalachians Revue,* among others. He studies, works, and lives in Chicago, IL. IG: @nicktakingpicsofstuff & Twitter: @nickwritinstuff

Iván Salí is a first-generation college student at California State University, Northridge earning a BA in English, Creative Writing. His work reflects the Nepantla state of mind. As an undocumented immigrant from Mexico City, he currently resides in Panorama City, a neighborhood in the San Fernando Valley, Los Angeles. IG: @ivansali_

Rick Smith is a clinical psychologist specializing in brain damage and domestic violence; he practices in Rancho Cucamonga, CA. He is a professional harmonica player who plays for The Mescal Sheiks, as heard on the soundtrack of the Academy Award-winning *Days of Heaven.* Recent books are *The Wren Notebook* (2000); *Hard Landing* (2010) and *Whispering In A Mad Dog's Ear* (2014), all from Lummox Press. His essay "Snowed In With Carl Sandburg" appeared in the 2019 issue of *Under The Sun.* Go to: docricksmith.com

SondriaWRITES is an Inland Empire-based freelance writer, author, and media content provider. She has released three short story collections, and is set to release her fourth: *The Carverians 2* in September 2020. Sondria also co-hosts The Black Book Club in Leimert Park, California.

Steele is a nonbinary communist poet from the Shenandoah Valley.

Mei Mei Sun was born in Yokohama, Japan, raised in Birmingham, Alabama, and now resides in Los Angeles. She lives with her tiny white puppy, numerous potted plants, and deep-seated trauma. Go to meimeisun.org.

Michelle "La Mousie" Vega. First-generation Chicanx artist from Chicago with a focus of exploring emotions/issues throughout illustrations such as vulnerability, agony, and pain; infusing modern-day Chicago gangbangers with West Coast elements. Her body of work consists of a storytelling concept challenging the male gaze while including various life experiences/stories that tie together the living experience in the space between the hyphen "Mexican-American." IG: @una.michelada

Megan Waring is a poet and playwright. She holds a BA in Creative Writing from Virginia Tech and is currently earning her MFA in Poetry from the University of Massachusetts Boston. Her work is forthcoming or published in *Salamander, Nailed Magazine, Mortar Magazine*, among others.

Aruni Wijesinghe is a project manager, substitute ESL teacher, occasional sous-chef, and erstwhile belly dance instructor. She is an emerging voice in the local literary community and has performed her work around Southern California. She lives a quiet life with her husband Jeff and their cats Jack and Josie.

Devynity Wray is a writer, visual artist & performer from South Jamaica, Queens, NY. She was a Nuyorican Poet's Cafe slam team member in 2002. Wray is a Cambridge Writer's Workshop alumna with a BA in Africana, Puerto-Rican/Latino Studies from Hunter College; she is currently in pursuit of an MFA in Visual Arts at Lesley University. Follow her at @devynitywray

Fernando Xáuregui is a translator and poet from La Puente, CA. He teaches literature and Spanish in the Cal State system.

Haolun Xu was born in Nanning, China. He immigrated to the United States in 1999 as a child and was raised in New Jersey. He spends his time between writing poetry and the local seashore.

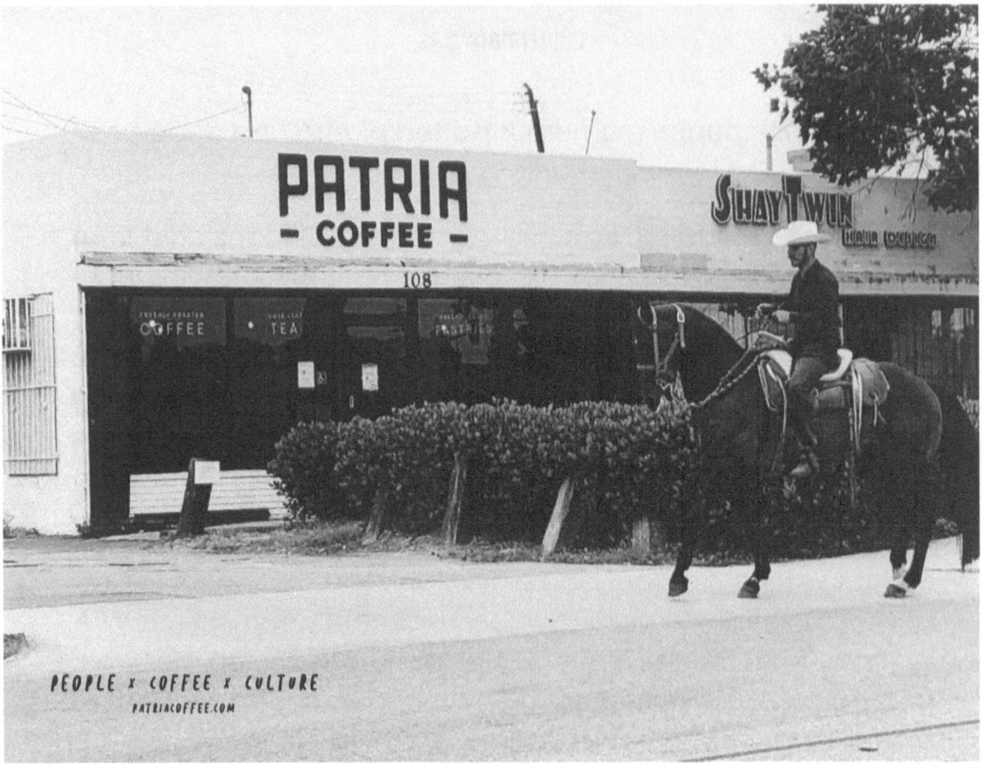
PATRIA
- COFFEE -
108
COFFEE
TEA
PASTRIES
PEOPLE x COFFEE x CULTURE
PATRIACOFFEE.COM

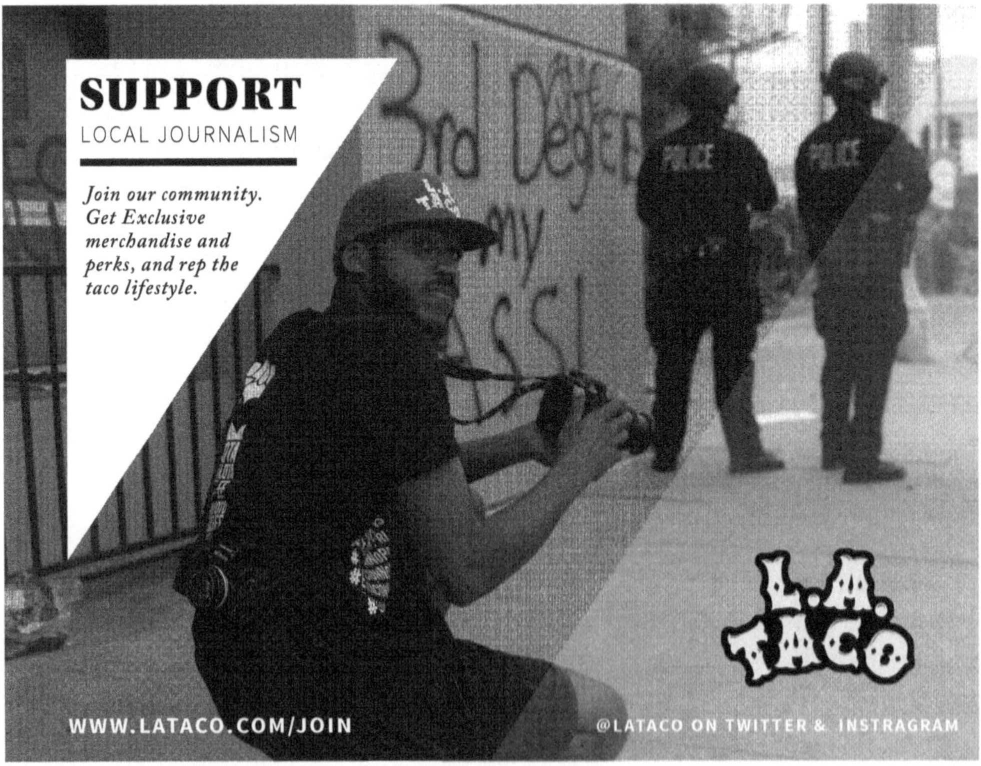
SUPPORT
LOCAL JOURNALISM
Join our community. Get Exclusive merchandise and perks, and rep the taco lifestyle.
POLICE
POLICE
L.A. TACO
WWW.LATACO.COM/JOIN
@LATACO ON TWITTER & INSTRAGRAM

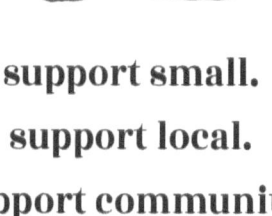

ÓRALE BOYLE HEIGHTS

Órale Boyle Heights is an interview podcast hosted by Erick Huerta. Tune in & listen to in-depth interviews with friends, foos, artists, and individuals doing amazing work in their communities

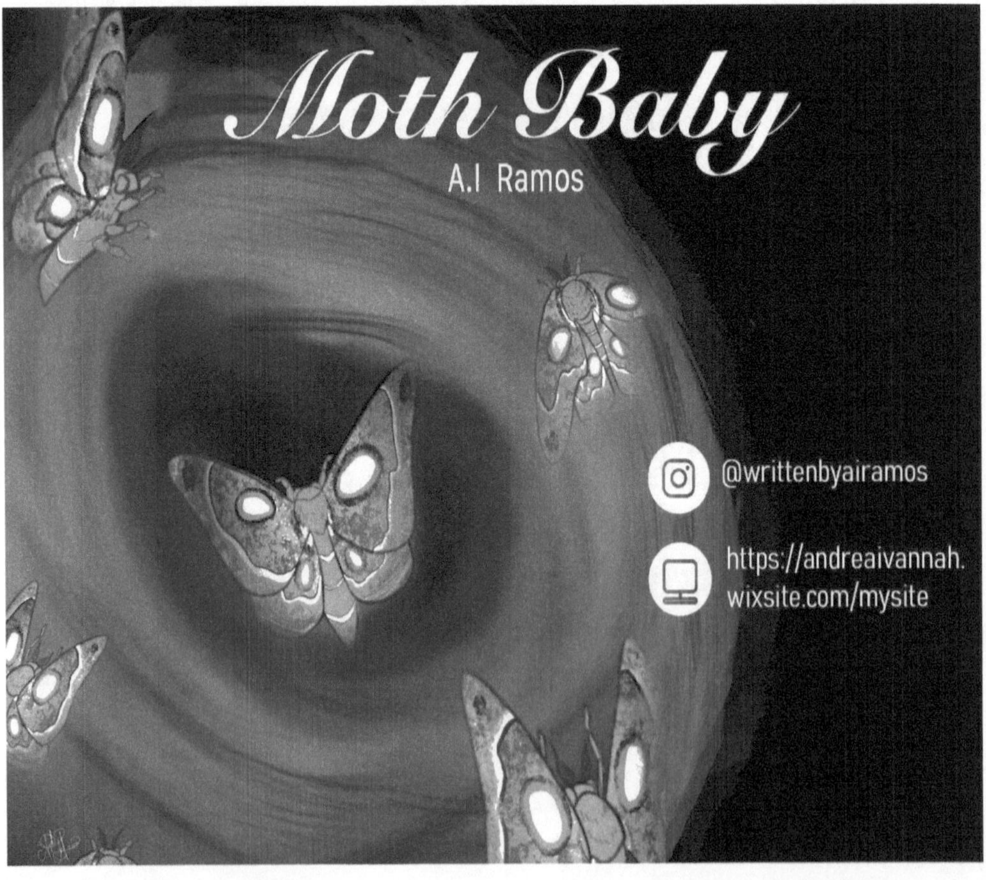

www.ingramcontent.com/pod-product-compliance
Lightning Source LLC
Chambersburg PA
CBHW031954010726
47493CB00007B/2195